# Sales Mastery

Proven Strategies and Psychological Tactics for Closing Deals

# Table of contents

INTRODUCTION. Who are you and why are you here? --- 4

Chapter 1. Every salesperson wants to know why customers don't buy from them. --- 7

Chapter 2. Talk Less, Sell More. --- 21

Chapter 3. A Simple Way to Understand Difficult Customer Decisions. --- 34

Chapter 4. Words and phrases that get in the way of selling. --- 52

Chapter 5. The Biggest Obstacles in Sales. --- 72

Chapter 6. The Most Common Mistake Salespeople Make. --- 83

Chapter 7. We make our own rules for talking to customers. --- 90

Chapter 8. Big Money Comes Faster. --- 101

Chapter 9. The Most Common Objection You Give Up On. --- 109

Chapter 10. What does it mean to milk a customer? --- 117

Conclusion. --- 125

# INTRODUCTION

## Who are you and why are you here?

Have you ever asked yourself why you are in sales? Why did you choose this career, this industry, this field? What drives you, what motivates you, what makes you get up every morning and go to work?

Maybe you will answer that you like to communicate with people, that you are good at persuading people, that you enjoy the process of negotiating and closing deals. Maybe you'll say that you want to help people solve problems, meet their needs, and improve their lives. Or maybe you'll say you just want to make a lot of money so you and your family can live comfortably and buy whatever you want.

All of these answers are true, but they are not perfect. They reflect your goals, desires, and ambitions, but not your true self. They talk about what you want to get out of the sale, but not what you want to get in return. They talk about what you do, not who you are.

So who are you? You are a salesperson. You are a professional. You are an expert. You are a leader. You are a winner.

You are the most important factor in every deal, in every sale. You are the one who creates value, offers solutions, demonstrates benefits, eliminates objections, and closes deals. You are the one who makes money for yourself, your team and your company.

You are here because you want to be the best at what you do. You want to increase sales, profits and revenue. You want to improve your skills, knowledge and abilities. You want to get rid of your fears, attachments and phobias. You want to overcome your weaknesses, mistakes and failures. You want to achieve your goals, dreams and aspirations.

You are here because you are ready to change. You are ready to change the way you think, behave and live your life. You are ready to let go of outdated beliefs, habitual prejudices and false illusions. You are ready to embrace new ideas, strategies and technologies. You are ready to step out of your comfort zone, break the mold, and escape the status quo.

You are here because you believe in yourself. You believe in your skills, talents and gifts. You believe in your worth, your uniqueness and your individuality. You believe in your mission, your vision and your passion. You believe in your strength, your will and your energy.

You are here because you want to get rich. Not just financially rich, but spiritually rich. Not just financially rich, but emotionally and socially rich. Personal riches and social riches. Not just to make yourself rich, but to make others rich.

You are here because you have chosen sales. Sales is not just a job, not just a business, not just a field. Sales is an art, a science, a philosophy. Sales is a way of self-expression, a way of self-realization, a way of self-improvement. Sales is your life. Welcome to sales.

# Chapter 1.

## Every salesperson wants to know why customers don't buy from them.

Welcome to the pages of a book on sales. Here you will learn why so many people fail in sales and don't make money. You will see that there are phobias. They prevent you from making money. With this book you will get rid of money phobia in any business. Let's talk about why you're here.

You probably want to increase your sales and profits. That's great, that's wonderful. I can help a lot of people who are winners. That's because I offer you the opportunity to not only learn, but to earn. Because everything I write here works in real life. Why are so many teachers, coaches, gurus and people in the business of selling information? Because it's all outdated and hasn't worked for a long time. For example, a long time ago I tried to sign up for sales training, but these people couldn't find anyone to train me with. So they told me to wait until they found people and recruited a group. They told me to wait until they had at least 10 people. And then we will let you know when the training starts.

This is complete nonsense. People who claim they can teach other people to sell can't sell training to other people who want it. And these people claim they can teach you to sell.

This book will show you how to make a lot of money.

I recommend that you share this information with your friends. Because if you share this information, it will become your memory and stay with you. Or it will disappear, like a dream that you remember when you wake up. But ten minutes later you forget it. And so it is with knowledge. If you do not share it, if you do not put it into practice, in two days you will forget it. It is the same with all the realizations that happen to you. I recommend that you share it with other people.

Don't take too long. If you can't apply it now, you have to start all over again. So if you're really determined to get rich. No more excuses. Mom is sick, you have to pick up your kid from school right away, a family vacation. You don't go. You don't go anywhere else. You make money. You make it right on your phone, without leaving your home or office.

Today, everyone is making money at home, on the computer, or on the phone. Millions and billions of dollars are made this way.

Procrastination and laziness lead directly to poverty. So if you don't want to be poor, you have to do something. The universe and the Lord God Himself will not help.

Without it, no money will come out. Because only when you make a sale, you have earned. Otherwise there is no way to get money. Only when you make a sale does it come, from other people, only when you make a sale. All the money is in the pockets of other people and all kinds of organizations. You cannot attract money any other way. Miracles don't happen. Miracles don't happen unless you make a sale. No rituals, prayers, amulets, figurines will help.

Business is about profit. Profit can only be made if you sell. Imagine a person who has money. He goes to London or New York, Bali or India. Some go to Switzerland with money, some go to India. Some go to Spain. The people who have a lot of money are the people you see on television. They came here to try to conquer the whole market. But they don't succeed. Because they don't know some of the secrets. And that's because of the way things work.

And you too can learn how to build your business, how to build your sales and how business works, how sales works. You can also do consulting. If you want to do that, it's a very profitable business. You can get results. If you can be accountable with your own money. I mean, if you say something and it works. If it doesn't work, the client gets their money back. If it works, you get your money back. You get your fee and everybody is happy. That's what business is about. Everybody wins and so do you.

Let's start with the first secret. You're constantly being told what to do. Read the project, with the right words, and sales will go through the roof. That's the only way they'll buy. But it won't help you if you don't know how to do it. At the top of the pyramid is the seller who is not afraid of the buyer. That's you, the one presenting the information. And a script you can download for free from the Internet won't help you. Why not? Because they won't believe you. And if you don't have anyone to sell to, there's no sale. If there's no one to sell to, there's no sale. If the person selling doesn't know how to talk, words, you can make the sale. You can become sothere's no sale. If he only knows what to say, the sale will not happen.

That's why we work to put you front and center from the very beginning.

You are the center of it. Why should you be rich? Why should people pay you? Why should they believe you? The reason sales don't happen is simple and straightforward. They don't believe you. Why should they believe you? When was the last time you believed in yourself?

Many of you have agreed to work for an unknown company that sells obscure things. In order to buy from them, you must be a Master Deal Maker. This is the person who handles the closing of the sales contract. This is the person who is trusted, who is an expert at solving people's problems, someone they turn to for help.

Think about it, what is sales?

You have to sell. It's not selling bread or meat or anything else. You can sell advice. You can sell information or you can sell problem solving. In fother words, if you believe you can solve a problem. If you can take responsibility for your words, you are hired primarily for sales. Without such people, any business doesn't work. Factories close, companies close. Thousands of people in different professions are out of work if the most important person who closes deals is not there. If a product doesn't sell, it's no good. Everyone who works there doesn't get paid.

The most important job in business is not the accountant, it's the person who closes the deals. Money is what everybody works for. Starting with the CEO, the boss, the owner. The owner and everybody else works for it. Without sales, the business does not happen.

So I want you to realize who you are.
You are the most important person in any business. You have to open the door with your foot. Because you are the only one who can bring money into this business. This business depends on you.
When you start to realize who you are and how to sell, everything starts to work. Even the scripts. Because you have a clear plan to figure out how to sell. And most importantly. You'll be free of ear. If the salesman is afraid of the product, is not sure about its quality, is afraid of his customer, then the sale is impossible.
Let's try to summarize who is the person who closes deals. You are the person who has to close the deal. So if you visualize yourself as the person who should and can close the deal, you will be fine. Congratulations, you are now starting to become a professional.
Now you won't have a problem selling. You will know who to sell to. How to attract people and how to weed them out. You'll even know how to weed out people you don't need to talk to.
Every business has three parts:
1. marketing (attracting customers);
2. selling a service or product
3. delivering the service

This book will introduce you to sales and all the intricacies of the profession. Here are some key aspects of being a successful salesperson. This book is designed to help you take your career to the next level or get your business off the ground.

The most important thing is to understand why people buy.

Every salesperson wants to know why customers don't buy from them. And the first thing to think about is what motivates people to spend money on your product. It's not a dream, a need, a problem, a pain, it's something you can influence now, even before you talk to the customer. Here are the factors you must consider when writing a proposal.

The first is price. It's no exaggeration to say that the cheaper the product, the easier it is to sell. But the relationship is not direct. In many industries, doubling the price only makes the seller's job 20% harder. This is not the case with ordinary goods. A seller of computer equipment should be on par with other companies in terms of pricing. Antique sellers, on the other hand, can raise prices. But only if they explain the reasons to the buyer. If you buy from them only because of the reduced price, it is an alarming signal that you can do nothing about. A low price offer will soon go up. And that often leads to low margins, and that's certainly not what we want.

The second thing to look for is quality. Clothing, appliances, medical and legal services. If you know that clothes are comfortable and hold their value over time, appliances will last for many years. Surgeries and medical procedures will be successful, and your rights will be protected on all sides. A $100,000 car has ten times the quality of a $10,000 car. When quality is at the forefront of your business, communication is paramount. After all, you need to explain to your customers why your product is better than the competition's.

If it's a service, you need to demonstrate competence. If it's a product, you need to explain its superiority. For example, durability, economy, and environmental friendliness.

Third is branding. In the beginning, the brand was simply a guarantee of quality. The name of the company was well known and people were satisfied with the quality of the products. Today, a brand is much more than that. It's a way of claiming to belong to a group of people who share a common point of view or possess certain qualities. So what's the secret sauce? People buy because they think it makes them look better in the eyes of others.

Fourth is choice. Today, you can buy almost anything on the major online shopping sites. Not every company needs a catalog with hundreds of pages. But people do need choice. Faced with so much choice, they will subconsciously think more about which product suits them better than whether you are worth working with. And fifth is convenience. How many times have you stopped at a gas station to get something to eat or drink, even though you know it costs more to get change than at the corner store? And how many times have you seen even a small line and walked out of the store without buying anything? Despite the huge selection of goods available at low prices. When companies ignore convenience, shoppers suffer and then find themselves without the goods, despite the obvious benefit to themselves. Online shopping thrives because it is convenient. Think about how much convenience the Internet and smartphones have brought to your life. Today, you can buy anything from apples to real estate with just a few clicks.

You don't even have to leave the house. Businesses that offer more convenience to the customer can immediately gain a greater advantage.

This can be summed up as follows. People are not robots, and they do not buy for one reason alone. Therefore, it is foolish to bet on just one reason. Analyze the supplier. Think about what qualities you are missing, how to fix them, and whether these qualities are needed in this situation. And start acting.

Solve customer problems and make money.

Now I'm going to talk about types of salespeople. These aren't really types of salespeople. They are people who think of themselves as salespeople.

The first type includes People who take orders and aren't really salespeople. People who work in retail. For example, at McDonald's, they take orders. "Give me this can of Coke, this bun." "Okay, what else do you want?" In other words, these people can be found in any store, any salon, they size up the product you like. They try it on and leave with their purchases.

The second type of people are those who call themselves salespeople. They are experienced, they sit back and do things the old-fashioned way. They're old-fashioned. They are not interested in new technology or social media. They're used to saying the same thing over the phone. They're not motivated, they're just doing their job.

And the third type is the salesperson, the most important type, the most influential and the most powerful type of salesperson.

But these are no longer salesmen. These are people of a much higher class. People who are respected and problem solvers. These are the people who can close deals. Until the deal is done, nothing else matters. You can do anything you want, you can dance and sing songs. But none of that's going to help. If the deal doesn't close, there's no sale.

So what's the difference between a salesman and a saleswoman?

The difference between a salesman and a master salesman is that people want to buy from him and solve their problems. And then the customer thinks he made the decision himself. The customer thanks him for what he did for them. In other words, this master salesman solved a very serious human problem. "We looked at all the options and found the best one for you." He never says, "Thank you for your purchase. When the deal is done, he says, "Congratulations. You have made a good and sound investment. You made the right choice. I just picked this for you." He has solved his customer's most global problem. The transaction is painless. It's nice and the person enjoys the process. He's not being told what to do. He's not being forced to buy something he doesn't need. The customer is offered the best option. And the person accepts it. That's the difference.

There is such a thing as a salesman. It's an order taker who works at McDonald's or a bakery. Bring me shoes this size. Bring me a coffee. Some salespeople don't know what a master salesman is. Old-fashioned without modern technology.

They continue to work the way they did thirty years ago. And sometimes they even make sales.

A master salesman is the top tier of salespeople who solve the most global problems. He doesn't force anyone to buy.

The person makes his own decision and thanks him for solving his global problem. In response, the salesman says to the person

"Congratulations, your life

"is much better now. Congratulations to you."

In this book you will learn unique information that will make you rich and successful. How to solve customer problems and make money.

Now you know who the sales masters are and why these people are considered the best salespeople. They don't need to convince, they don't need to push, they don't need to be tricky. Their weapon of choice is the famous "offer you can't refuse". Because they solve problems. Quickly, effectively, and permanently.

Don't mistake enthusiasm for softness. Inexperienced salespeople are so eager to solve problems that they mistake wishful thinking for reality. Then they are surprised by the lack of sales growth and become disillusioned with the business itself. All you have to do is think and realize that your customer doesn't live only by his problems. Everything, his desires, can be categorized.

Dreams. Whether it's a limousine, a new Ferrari, a trip to Antarctica or a trip on a spaceship, dreams come in many forms, but they have one thing in common. They are never urgent. They have an extremely low priority.

The fulfillment of dreams is put off until later. That "later" could be months or even years from now. If your product is just someone's dream, they won't buy it now.

Demand. What the buyer wants to buy in the near future. Like a dream, it's not urgent yet. But it is already important. For example, a buyer realizes that he needs warm boots at the beginning of winter. He will definitely buy them, but not in the summer. He has a more urgent need. He has time to think and choose the most appropriate style of boots.

A problem. An important and urgent one. If he ignores it, the situation will get worse. To prevent a negative situation, he is ready to buy without paying attention to what is happening here and now. For example, a person rushing to an important meeting and caught in the rain is willing to pay double the price for an umbrella so as not to ruin an expensive suit. This happens because it costs more to negotiate.

Pain. This is a problem that should have been solved yesterday. A negative situation has arisen and no one will bargain and pay the same price to fix it or at least do less damage. For example, you had a leaky faucet for a long time, but you never got around to fixing it. And one fine morning the water bursts and drowns the lower apartments. You pay double the price of a plumber just to get the problem fixed quickly.

The dream of selling sounds nice. If you want to become a master salesman, you have to deal with needs. But the most ideal are problems and pains. Just learn to look at each situation and understand what needs you will have to deal with.

We must shift our focus. Selling houses instead of mortgages, health instead of medicine, heat instead of heaters. There is certainly a positive side to this idea. It focuses the buyer's attention on the benefits they will receive. However, the sales assistant helps to solve the problem. In the pursuit of a positive image, it is easy to forget this fact. That's what the average salesperson does. Why delve into the customer's problems when you can talk about the benefits of a product or service by the book? After all, if you didn't, most businesses would simply go out of business. But thinking about yourself without thinking about your customers, talking about the benefits of your product without getting into your customers' problems, is like putting on your shoes and then your pants. It will probably work, but it's a very hard process. Let's take a speaker system as an example. For a simple salesman, the situation is very simple. He gives the customer a lot of information. A master salesman, on the other hand, realizes that the problem is always multifaceted. One customer for a small apartment. The second is a large club, the third is not price sensitive but needs special modifications for outdoor concert venues. Put yourself in the customer's shoes and compare the two scenarios: In the first case, you are bombarded with a lot of unnecessary information. Maybe there was a necessary option, but the customer can't pick it out of this pile of words. In the second, you are asked a few simple questions and then offered the exact way to solve the problem here and now.

This is where you pay for the product or service. Don't expect the customer to start telling you about their problem on their own. After all, they are not masters of the perfect deal. They are shy about talking about their problems and don't know what they want. You must not only know what the problem is, but also show it to the client. You are the doctor, the customer is the patient, the problem is the diagnosis, the product is the cure.

Solve the problem or pain, not the desire. Most offers are made in situations that really can't be refused. Problems are almost always the starting point of the deal. Learn to identify problems, categorize them, and offer solutions. Yes, it's harder than copying a template. But it has an impact and brings benefits.

# Chapter 2.

## Talk Less, Sell More.

People often tell me that I'm not a very social person. I'm an introvert. I like to sit quietly, mind my own business, and not talk to anyone. But when I have to make a sale or a transaction, I talk. So it's a choice. There's no such thing as an introvert or an extrovert. So if you choose to be an introvert, you can do business. Congratulations. You're going to have a successful life. I say that with confidence.

The most influential people in sales are introverts. The secret is why. It's not about what you say to your customers. It's about listening to your customers. What their problems are and what they need to solve. That's why some companies have a contest for $10,000, $100,000 for $1 million in sales. To win that contest, you have to prove that you're making a certain amount of money in commissions. It's not about how much product you sell. It's about how much commission money you make. This is very important. Nobody likes to sell for pennies. They want to be rich and successful. With that money you can buy anything you want.

But the most powerful tool in sales is silence. Another secret is the 80/20 rule. Twenty percent of the time you speak. You ask questions. You clarify the situation. The person asking the questions is the one in control. Let them talk. Give the client the opportunity to say what they feel they need to say. Your job is to listen and learn to listen. A very useful way to do this is to close your eyes and listen to your customers.

How they breathe, how they speak and at what speed. Many people take in information at the same rate as they speak. Your job is to listen first and ask clarifying questions. So sometimes your best tool is to remain silent. Then the person you are talking to can ask, "Can you hear me? "Yes, I just need to think about it for a minute," you reply. As a salesperson, you often hear this objection: "I need to think about it. Can't we say the same thing? You need to think and take a moment to pause, and that will help turn the situation in your favor. And think about whether or not your product is a good fit for this person? You need to think about whether you want to spend your time with this person? Control the situation by asking questions. More than eighty percent of the time, the customer is talking in great detail about the product or service they need. And you should ask questions to clarify the details. And don't think that the more you talk, the more you sell. The more you overwhelm a person with information, the more you hurt yourself. The best salesperson in the world is your client. Your customer is the only person who can talk himself into buying your product. Your job is to help him, to lead him to that decision with questions. This is very important because every time someone asks you, "How much does it cost? You answer that you would like to start by asking a few clarifying questions about the order quantity, quality, special technical specifications for operation ..... "We will find the best option for you and calculate the price". In other words, you ask questions that reveal the customer's needs.

If you answer questions off the top of your head, you will hurt both yourself and the customer. Because you don't know what he needs. He needs a $1,000 product or a $10,000 product. How can you answer that question if you haven't identified the need? For example, if the person says, "I need delivery today. You answer, "You want to buy this product if we deliver it today, right? Yes?" The customer says, "Yes, I do." That's the person deciding that your product is right for them. You can use that to close the deal. He's already made his decision. You haven't done anything.

Otherwise, you are no different than an online store where everything is written. Your product has this price. It takes a week to ship. All the specifications are in the description. Here's the video.

Why do we need you? To find out what a person needs and how they need it, and to get money from your customers. If you don't realize this, you are no different than an online store, it works 24 hours a day, so it will sell more. As a rule, insecure people always try to say too much. This is how insecurity manifests itself. Confident people ask questions. So your job is to ask questions and talk less.

The golden rule is 80-20. You talk 20% and your client answers 80% of your questions. That way, the person has to tell you the real problems they have. And they will pay you for solving the real problem they have.

Talk less, sell more.
Talking to customers does not mean that you have total control over the conversation.

On the contrary, now you will learn how to get what you want without saying too much, just by listening and asking the right questions.

To say something, you must first listen. But here's the problem: most people listen to each other without listening to what they have to say. At best, out of politeness, they listen to what the other person is going to say before they say anything of their own. This is a problem in everyday life, but in business the damage alone can be enormous. So learn how to listen.

Let's take the following rules to heart.

Never interrupt. We are taught this from childhood, but apparently it is not enough. After all, you always want to show that you understand what the other person is thinking. But be careful. No one likes to be interrupted, even with good intentions. It is a blatant disrespect for others. Those who sense this attitude will be more reluctant to speak directly. This is the rule of a true master salesperson.

Focus. Not all customers are succinct. Some customers talk themselves to death. In this case, it's easy to get distracted by the meaningless chatter on the phone and think about your own. Whether it's an upcoming dinner, a long-awaited party at a friend's house, or an unexpected problem. But if you get distracted, you're bound to miss something important. And if you don't listen carefully, your buyer is likely to notice your distraction and put an end to your intended transaction.

Make them feel comfortable. No, don't make them feel like they're talking to an old coworker. But don't be indifferent, either.

When selling offline, keep eye contact. Remember to nod often. Smile when appropriate. If it's a phone call, say "yes," "sure," "okay," and similar words. Listening does not mean being completely disinterested.

Show compassion. No matter how much you would like to see a person's pockets stuffed with money, he is first and foremost a human being. Understand this, or the road to becoming a master salesman will be closed to you. Let go of your preconceived notions, look at things through his eyes, and understand what his point of view is based on. That's what dialogue is all about. Read between the lines. Delve into the customer's problem as if it were your own. Then your answer will be right on target.

Don't stigmatize a person. Everyone has their own hurtful stereotypes. Don't label people. Dumb, stupid, uneducated, stupid, shy, talks too quietly or shouts too loudly. You may quickly convince yourself that you don't want to do business with this person, or they won't buy anything. But an "uneducated" person can make a lot of money, and a "mumbler" can sometimes close deals worth millions. Be tolerant of other people's imperfections. After all, you are not marrying them.

Watch and listen carefully. On the phone, you listen with your ears only. In face-to-face communication, your eyes come into play. Even if you're not a psychologist, you can pick up signals by observing a client's body language and facial expressions. The eyes can tell you so much about the meaning of what the person you're talking to is saying.

And you'll almost automatically be able to figure out what's really bothering the client and what they're talking about. Not to mention the fact that they may be lying.

Don't jump to conclusions. Do you know why you often don't listen to the person you're talking to? It's because you've already heard all the important points. Or rather, we think we've heard them. There is certainly a reason for this. Most customers provide the most important information in a short period of time. However, in the rest of the piece, which should be devoid of content, there is sometimes hidden information that can completely turn the tide. A single sentence is all it takes to make the picture absolutely clear.

Don't just keep quiet, sometimes give in and try to do everything as calmly as possible. The winner is not the one who has a more powerful weapon, but the one who is able to get to the core of the problem, understand the client's motivation, choose the right moment and make the right request. Yes, at first it will be hard for you to listen to a person calmly. But the effort will pay off in a short time.

Once you've learned how to listen, it's time to learn how to talk.

In this life as a master of sales, you will never set a salary, even if you really like the boss. Because you set your own salary. In any company where you work as a master salesman, there is no ceiling. But there's no floor. There's no floor, there's an abyss under your feet. If you fall into it, unfortunately, you are in big trouble. So as an entrepreneur, the first thing you have to know is. As a businessman or salesman.

Where to get potential customers. That is, the person you want to sell to.

How to use social media to buy customers. Buying is so easy and simple these days. You can sign up on Google Facebook, Instagram, YouTube, etc. Set up ads there where you can list a portrait of your buyer persona. I want people of this age, with this hobby. And your ads will provide you with customers around the clock.

How to sell better and better? The first thing you need to do is to fix your subconscious mind, which always keeps people away from the subject of wealth. People who have achieved great success and great wealth have all been master salesmen and very closed people. Steve Jobs and Elon Musk, Bill Gates. These are the ones that come on the scene. They appear on television. To promote their companies and businesses. They talk. Most of them are silent in life, and they're good at it.

You need to learn how to do it. You have to understand what makes them make the big money. Now we're going to find out how to do it. How to communicate effectively. You have to know these statistics and rules. In one-on-one visual communication. 55% of the information a person shows with their body and facial expressions. 38% is tone of voice, pauses. And only 7% of information is conveyed through speech with words. Information is images, tone of voice and words. But in a telephone conversation, 80 percent is tone. And only 20 percent is the words you say.

Realize how important this is. Think about speaking with the right intonation.

Try saying the same words with different intonations. I want you to imagine how you feel. Say the same sentence over and over again. "Hello. What can I do for you?" The intonation and the feelings it evokes. Your job is to speak confidently and clearly. Confident and clear so that you don't annoy anyone. So that people don't get annoyed, so that they don't feel stupid. Yes, in other words, your job is for people to talk to you and realize that you are a professional and a problem solver at the highest level. That there is a solution and you have it. That's what you sell for money. Your job is also to start listening to yourself. It is recommended that you record your conversations with people. Everybody has a telephone, there is a machine called a voice recorder. It is a machine that records sound and record yourself when you talk to someone. Just turn on the recorder and listen to yourself talking to someone in a certain tone of voice. Close your eyes and ask yourself if you are sure of what you are saying. Where did your voice shake? At what point did your intonation go up or down? Intonation always goes up when you are being asked. It always goes down when you're speaking. And when you're speaking neutrally, it stays at the same level. You can manipulate your intonation.

 The first thing to do is to pay attention to your intonation. The next thing is to listen to your own voice. Listen to yourself and the other person's voice. Your intonation should match the speed of the other person. When your speed and intonation match, people will understand you because they are listening to your voice.

This gives you more tools to influence the sale. You will get even closer to being a master salesperson. You will be able to make limited money.

Now that you've learned how to listen, it's time to learn how to talk. It doesn't matter what you say, it's how you say it. But once you understand this, you'll know how to make a magical connection with your clients.

Persuasive presentation tips.

Let's say that again. The tone of your voice is far more important than the words you speak. In other words, it's time to realize that your voice is a tool, and it's time to learn how to use it. The way you speak is your calling card. People hear your voice on the phone and visualize you. It would be foolish to underestimate its importance in face-to face communication. Your voice will be heard if you follow these principles.

The first is speech rate. This refers to the speed at which you speak, the length of your words, and your pauses. Speaking rate depends on your personality, emotional state, and the context in which you are communicating. Confident people speak at a steady, moderate pace with clear pauses between words.

Inexperienced salespeople may think that speaking fast is the best way to be expressive, but it's not. On the contrary, speaking too fast is a sign of nervousness and is often perceived as such. Of course, speaking too fast can lead to a loss of meaning and focus.

However, slowing down should be done skillfully. First, don't overdo it so that it doesn't sound like you're slowing down. Second, make sure it does not sound preachy. Either can irritate the other person. It is also necessary to maintain a steady pace of speech when dealing with complex issues or when the listener needs time to understand.

Volume. Don't talk about situations that make you raise your voice, such as poor cell phone service or noise in the room. We're interested in the psychological and emotional factors. After all, the volume of your voice is a tool that ensures not only the appropriateness of the communication situation, but also the expressiveness and variety of your speech. And this is where beginners are at risk. For example, since childhood we have been told about the voice of the commander. In fact, the intensity of the voice, the increase in volume, increases the distance between you and your interlocutor. Of course, this way of speaking can also be perceived as insecurity. Remember these tips every time you speak to someone.

Tone and pitch. These concepts are always easy to confuse, so let's start with the basics. Voice pitch refers to the ability to produce low or high notes. Timbre, on the other hand, is the individual coloration of the voice created by additional vibrations. Tone is automatic and requires practice. A low voice gives confidence to your speech, while a high voice means you are not in control of yourself. In addition, a decent voice not only makes a good impression on the listener, but also sets the mood and conveys confidence.

Intonation. Few people know how to use 10 different tones to communicate.

But they certainly know how to say the same sentence and give it different meanings. Intonation allows the other person to catch your mood and the hidden meaning of your phrase; it is a tool for creating the right melody and thus capturing the other person's attention.

The clearer and more varied your intonation, the more powerful your speech will sound. Monotonous intonation can give the impression of formality and undermine efforts to establish rapport. It is important to choose a medium depth of intonation and a smooth transition from one tone to another.

Silence. Silence sometimes indicates that you are not satisfied with what you have heard. But meaningful pauses between sentences enhance the importance of what is being said. Silence is really gold when you learn how to use pauses. Because the right pause emphasizes the climax of your speech, ensures that what you hear reaches the other person, and shows that you are in control of the conversation. It's better to use a well-planned pause to summarize your thoughts than to use silly phrases.

Semantic emphasis. To focus the other person's attention on the right words, use all the tips above. You can emphasize words by saying them slowly, loudly, in a slightly different rhythm, or by pausing. The method is not important. What is important is that you emphasize the right words and that you do it correctly. The words appear to have the same semantic purpose. In fact, different shades of phrasing can be very appropriate at different stages of a negotiation.

The more you listen, the more you will notice this difference.

Simple linguistic rules will make your job easier. Use them to emphasize important information effectively and unobtrusively.

There are many rules. But fortunately, these rules are very simple and focus on simple rules or naturalness. Just get out of your cage, get rid of your misconceptions, and stop talking. Then you will soon sound confident. And you will find yourself on the path to real confidence.

# Chapter 3.
# A Simple Way to Understand Difficult Customer Decisions.

Answer yourself honestly. Would you allow a surgeon with no training or experience to operate on you? In other words. Would you allow a stranger to operate on you? They go into your body and mess with it. A reasonable person probably wouldn't. But many people start a business with no training, no skills, no experience, no education. The same thing happens in sales.

Do you think you can do sales without the training required for the profession?

It's a very questionable profession. Even more questionable than entrepreneurship. Because nobody can explain who an entrepreneur is and what he does. But think about it. What are your chances of success? But the truth is that selling is a very powerful tool and very powerful. You can make more than a surgeon, more than a teacher.

There are benefits to working in sales. You are working for a new company, and like all companies, you need a sales professional. There are no exceptions in any business. Everyone needs someone to close the deal, someone to solve other people's problems. I'll say it again. You are the one who solves people's problems. They are valued, and why? The sales master led the customer to a decision, the best decision of their life.

Let's talk about who you are. Simply put, it's who you are and how you communicate and treat people.

You can treat them down or you can be on equal footing with your customer. Unfortunately, many salespeople consider themselves inferior when interacting with a customer. For whatever reason, they start licking their lips and begging. In other words, they start the conversation with the customer from a position of inferiority. The property was for sale and the client came in like a king. Where exactly does it hurt? What medicine have you been taking?" Why does He says show me all the options that are on the market today. And this person is like a personal chauffeur, he just drives the car and takes the client to all the properties. This salesman believes that the client is the boss, the head of his life. And he just obeys. He acts like an order taker. With this attitude you lose all influence and become a pauper. You have to put your communication with the client on the right basis from the very beginning. Otherwise, you will lose leverage, lower your status, and look like a beggar.

What is the best frame of reference? Relationships. Every relationship has its own frame of reference. In other words, you have your own balloon. When communication takes place, one balloon absorbs the other. For example, a galaxy absorbs another galaxy and they merge and become one. The same thing happens in every relationship. In other words, the stronger ball wins. It has to be the one that sells.

There are two people who are buyers. Because there are two sales going on. One sells to one, the other sells to the other. But the one who wants to help the other one wins. That's how it should always be. The buyer tried to convince you that I don't have the money. I have to think about it and something else.

To interact from the beginning, you have to take a stand. The best frame is called the doctor's frame. The person who heals. In other words, what happens? Suppose you go to the doctor and you have some problem. The doctor comes out and says, "We've been waiting for you for so long. Welcome. Today you can get three treatments for the price of one. Also, today you'll get your medicine for free.

If you get the situation right from the beginning. You immediately strengthen your position. How does the doctor talk to you? You have a problem and you go to him. He starts talking to you very calmly. And most importantly, what does he do? The doctor asks you questions. The one who's in control is the one who asks the questions. "What is your problem? "What is bothering you? "My leg hurts." "You say it's been hurting for a couple of days. He's identifying the problem. And the doctor is never selling you anything. He gives you a prescription for medicine. And his recommendations for a week, for example. That means no football. And then you follow the doctor's instructions. And soon your health improves dramatically. Nobody says, "I'll give you a discount, I'll operate on you much cheaper." You need a doctor because you have a problem. I need a doctor so I don't have pain, so I don't have a problem. Nobody tells the doctor, "I have money, save me. Take the money and serve me.

I want to say, very importantly, don't be dependent on anything in this sale. Never put yourself in the position of the asker. That is your positioning, your frame. In other words, nothing in your life depends on this sale.

My life doesn't depend on it at all, even if I don't have money to buy food today. Why is that? No one likes to buy from people in need. The reason is that the doctor is always in a high position. He is always the authority and the helper. Everyone relies on him and it depends on the case. Money that has no value, for me in this case, when my leg hurts. I can't define things. And that's my problem.

Solving problems for the patient or potential or potential customer is a core value. Money can't solve the problem. So when you're selling, when you're working for a company, first of all you have to believe that you're the best salesperson. You have to believe that you're selling high quality products that really work. That really solve problems. And most importantly, you have to use what you sell. For example, you work in car sales. And you don't like Rolls-Royce, you prefer BMW.

You should not sell Rolls-Royce. You should have a dream in life to buy a Rolls-Royce. Maybe you don't have that kind of money right now. But it should be the finest car. For you, there is no better car in the world. Only then would you really know all the characteristics of your product. And you would tell it like it is. Because that's what you want. And you would tell him or her the same dream. And it should be realized in his or her life. Because he has money. He can't afford not to realize it. Otherwise you're like a thief trying to steal a client's money.

If you don't think you work for the best company in the world, selling the best product in the world, the best goods in the world.

Go to another company today. Because you can't sell that. If you don't believe in the product, you're not going to be the best, you're not going to be number one. If you don't want to buy it.
Your job is to make people want to buy it in the first place. Make this decision work for you. You should be jealous of those who buy.
The things you sell every day, they do a lot of business. You should envy them and congratulate them. You want to buy it too, but now you have to save up for it. Congratulations, it's a great product.
That is the attitude you should have toward the product. If you have any doubts and you think you're not working for the best company in the world, quit right now. Find a company where everything works to your satisfaction. When you go home, be proud that you work for the best company in the world. Where real problems get solved. And people are happy when they give you their money. Only then can you sell your product to anyone. So how you start interacting with people is very important.
The atmosphere around you is you. You solve people's problems for money. You are the master of selling. Money, but it's just paper. It's just paper in your bank account, just a number. And you have something that makes life better. You believe in it. You have a responsibility, and you have a responsibility to ask questions about what you need to learn. And if you ask the right leading questions, you can help the person you're talking to know that you have what they need.

When you do this, everyone is happy because the customer is listening and getting exactly what they need. They are satisfied that you have solved their problem. It is very important not to speak from a subordinate position, no matter who you are talking to. The best frame of reference is the solver of huge, grandiose problems, and that is the reference point. How, in what tone, and in what position an interaction begins is how it happens. So don't ask people to buy from you, but be a world-class professional master salesperson.

Why is a control system important?
You have your own bottom line, just like your client. You didn't know it before, but now you can gain a deeper understanding of the intricacies of the relationship and take control of the process.
A simple way to understand your customer's complex decisions. The Three-Box Strategy is simple and solves the problem of choice. With it, you don't need to be an expert psychologist to get the customer to buy and win the next deal. However, if you want to be more effective, you need to delve deeper into the psychology of choice and learn additional techniques.
Choice or Failure. Our lives are made up of choices. They can be as small as "what sweets or cookies would be good for afternoon tea" or as large as "which city to buy a house in. Regardless of the scale, choosing is a whole process with a complex structure that is influenced by many factors.

Choosing the best option may seem like a simple task, but life is much more complicated.
 We'll talk about the intricacies later, but for now let's understand the basics. Choice always requires the presence of several alternatives and sufficient desire. Human values are many, the most important being money, time, pleasure, love, comfort, and life itself. Lack of choice is very frustrating for a person. Therefore, when people delay making important decisions, they feel uncomfortable. This is similar to the feeling of insecurity when you remember the wrong decisions you made a long time ago. But at the same time, as a master of sales, you should realize that deep in a person's soul, he is ready to make a decision or has already made it.
 Why is it that everyone is afraid to make a choice? Often the choice is "keep the status quo or change it. All things being equal, it seems easier and safer to keep things as they are. After all, you don't have to leave an (often imagined) comfort zone or disrupt an imagined stability. Most importantly, there is no need to do anything. The choice between "action" and "inaction" is simple.
Change is always a step into another world. Even win-win situations have their hidden problems. These can cause anxiety and fear. In a business relationship, a client can never be completely sure of your integrity, the quality of your product, or that it will deliver the results he wants. He will value what he has in his hand, no matter what treasure you offer. As a result, the client often finds a compromise in the word "later. In other words, he's fooling himself and he's fooling you.

After all, nobody refuses to buy. Just better tomorrow, after he gets a paycheck or consults with his wife, he will undoubtedly make a decision. After all, he's not in a hurry. He can be patient, and so can you, it seems. Another problem is the lack of understanding of the meaning of payment itself. Buying something is certainly profitable, and people perceive it as an investment. In the other case, they see the need to pay as a tribute and associate themselves as victims. A classic example is utilities. Everyone perceives such charges as an unfair punishment and sometimes as exorbitant costs. Although commercial products are not threatened by this undesirable trend, prejudices do arise.

In addition, the customer perceives the purchase not only as a gain, but also as a loss. Loss of other opportunities. If they buy real estate in one city, they believe that they are unlikely to be able to buy something in another city. When you put money into an investment, you are mentally saying goodbye to buying your dream yacht in the near future. While talking to you, he will think about your competitors and their favorable conditions. People tend to regret even those opportunities they may never take advantage of.

Help your clients overcome the fear of choice. Start with the good stuff. You have to deal with what is often called simple choice. This involves analyzing multiple alternatives based on understandable criteria and then deciding on the best option. This task is more obvious than semantic choice, which requires people to create their own criteria, and even more obvious than personal choice, which concerns their future destiny.

Most of the fears that clients insist on can be overcome by using the following few techniques:

Approach the other person. The other person is looking for what they call their comfort zone. Show them the illusory nature of their comfort zone. Formulate a scenario that the prospect doubts. Without my product, they will lose money, health, safety and other values. They can clearly see the future and will regret their past decisions. You have the truth, and there is no need to exaggerate, much less invent.

Always leave them a way out. If you don't like it, I'll give you your money back," a statement that has been used dozens of times to sell products and services with conviction. After all, customers can make a difference if they want to. That's why millions of people around the world buy without trying on clothes, or buy items from online stores at amazing prices. Don't be afraid to give them their money back. Because I'm confident in my product. You should have confidence in your product.

Don't let the word "later" fool you. It's true that sometimes buyers think about an offer and come back. But more often than not, they walk away and never come back. Try to categorize all the reasons respondents put off buying. In other words, explain that procrastination is not worth it. The perfect time will never come, money is always tight, and there will always be doubts. But if the customer buys now, you will soon feel the fruits of your decision.

Choices aren't as scary as customers make them out to be.

They turn simple decisions into complex ones, and into the most important decisions of their lives.

To do this, you must free a person from fabricated fears, set the record straight, and present two scenarios. Most importantly, you must deliver more value than the asking price. The greater the difference between value and price, the easier it will be for you to convince them. Which strategy to use? The choice is yours.

Let's talk about a very serious problem and dilemma. People can't make the decision to sell for a high price or to sell for a low price. Why it matters. How much you sell a product for is how much you make. Unless you make a life-changing decision, you will never make good money. Let's take the first example. Let's say you get 100 applications, that's 100 customers over the course of a month. Let's say you sell a product for $100. You have 50% of the people buying from you, then you will make 5000 dollars in a month. If you want to get rich. Sell something for 10,000 dollars. You talk to 100 customers on the phone 100 times a month. But only two people actually buy. In other words, two people out of 100 are interested in your product, your service, whatever it is. Two people paid $10,000 each. That's $20,000 a month. You've done the same absolute work and asked the same number of questions to the same number of people. But you made 400 percent more. So you're making more money. That's right.

People who buy for more money have less problems. Those people are thinking for themselves, they're making their own decisions, they're making their own sales.

It's always easy to sell expensive things for higher prices. They're not going to haggle over a Ferrari. They come in and say I need one. The deal is made and they leave. People who can afford to buy for $100,000 have a lot less trouble. So a two percent statistic is more successful than you selling for $100. Your job is to position yourself. How much you want to make. You have to realize from the beginning that selling high is always more profitable than selling low. You will network with other people. They have a different attraction. You have more interesting problems and more interesting contacts. You will make more interesting acquaintances. You can make connections. Let's say you've been working at a Ferrari dealership for ten years. What are your contacts? You're going to meet them in the course of your work. Think about it. It's more interesting to sell yachts and airplanes. One deal a year might be enough. Think about what you like best, what's more interesting to you? If you waste your time on trivial things. You won't be happy. Is that what you want? You'll never be happy that way. You already know that you have to sell at a higher price.

Can you make more money?
But there are people who can't pay $10,000. Then sell something not for $10,000, but a similar product for $5,000. The next step is to sell to people who can only afford to pay $1,000. There's an economy option for them too.
The idea is this.
Start with $10,000 dollars. To everyone who can afford it.

And create additional products to offer people to buy them. If you sell one product, it's just yes or no. If you sell two products, one for $10 and one for $5, there's a lot to choose from. And if you have three products in your product line, it's even more interesting. This product is VIP, this one is intermediate and this one is for beginners. Give them a choice. Start with expensive products and work your way down. In other words, from expensive to less expensive.

I want your life to flourish. I want you to enjoy it and make a lot of money. And I want you to live the life you've always dreamed of.

Poverty has signs. Poverty has signs of poverty. Poverty has talismans to attract luck and money. Things that supposedly attract luck. It is very important today to put all these things in a garbage bag and throw them away. You will become a beggar because all these signs are poverty talismans. They attract poverty rather than repel it. It is important to understand these things. If you are not a tool for attracting money, wealth and happiness. You have simply given your power to these charms. You have surrendered your destiny to cheap goods. You have surrendered your ability to earn, to control your life to these things. Elon Musk, Bill Gates and other billionaires have done nothing of the sort. We should at least emulate those who have already achieved something. They don't need a mascot. If you have these things, you immediately become lower in status. Lower than the object you've given power over your life to. I want you to remember. What you gave up and what you gave power to. You can't be an entrepreneur.

Because you have given all your power to things that you have bought in the marketplace.

What is money? I don't need money. I need results that money can buy. That's health, love, happiness. These are all things that money can buy. If you think money can't buy health, you're wrong. Most marriages break up because of financial problems. Because they don't have a chance in this world. People with money can afford things. Yes, women are biologically like that. They are calmer and want to have children with a man who will provide for them. Without money, we can't procreate. I talk about love and wealth as happiness because without them you can't procreate.

You either believe you can get rich or you don't. I want you to believe that you can be rich. Because you now have the most powerful tools to change yourself that will work in your business. You will be able to easily take money from your clients for your work. You will become fearless and confident.

Different prices and different offers. This is the three box technique. For example, you go to Macdonald's and there are small, medium and large fries and Coca Cola. That's what happens in the human mind. You don't choose yes or no. You choose a version. In other words, you choose a version of a proposition. You choose the one that best suits your needs. When we offer something cheaply, we're offering it to people who won't buy it at an expensive price.

But that offer doesn't quite satisfy the buyer in terms of quantity and quality. That's why you put out a product that nobody buys. Let's say you make an even more attractive product.

It has everything. Most people will buy it. Then you make a VIP offer. And it's more likely to be bought by 10 percent. It depends on what you're selling, but start there. If you create the illusion that they have a choice, then people will buy. But your main goal is to sell a mid-priced product. That's the product that 50 percent of your customers are going to buy. Your job is to sell that product. You make a very expensive product, so average seems like a good option. Oddly enough. People who think they need VIP will buy it. And the third product has to live up to its value. It has to be something, it has to exceed its price. Someone will want to try to check out a scam or not.

After the cheap product, people will want to buy the mid-range product. I'll say this again because it's very important. This product that you're making, the mid-range product, is a little bit above what the market demands. It's much more powerful. And you have to make sure that people buy that product. This product is your flagship, and it has to deliver everything you promised your customers. The middle product should solve all the problems. Because it solves the customer's core problem and need. You can't force people to buy the most expensive product. But you can divide the product into a first part and a second part. If a person buys the first part, he will definitely buy the second part. Because it is logical. If you want to sell one product, add two more. Organize your offer in a clear and simple way to increase sales of the main product and make additional profit. These ingenious techniques are simple and therefore effective. Try them and you will be convinced.

Now you have the Three Box Technique. And now you can start selling expensive things. And the person will buy it.

How to Make More Money Faster. You've learned how to make more money and save time by selling high-value products and services. This is a universal technique that can change not only your business, but your life. Use it as soon as possible.

Pricing Strategies. Almost all salespeople feel uncomfortable quoting a price. Then they are asked, "Why is your price so high?" and they panic. They feel the symptom of "hustle" when they think the price is too high, and these feelings are passed on to their customers. But how do you know your price is too high? Because you don't know where the prices come from or how they're calculated. It's time to fix that. The cost of producing a product and the markup. A hundred years ago, it was the norm to add 10-15% profit to the cost price. Those who sell a unique product, not heaters, should not consider the competition. Doctors may charge $10 or $100 an hour for their services, but that doesn't mean the best services come from a cheap doctor.

Packaging is important. I don't mean a pretty box, but product packaging in a broader sense. In other words, it's about how you communicate value and whether that value outweighs the price in the eyes of a potential buyer. When you see so much useful stuff packed into a product, you can't help but think, "This is better than anything I've ever seen. If this is just the budget version, what's in the full version? Now you can put any price tag on it and no one will ask why it's so expensive.

The value will exceed any price tag.

Brand value. And in our world, brands win. The most important thing about a watch is not the accuracy of the time, but simply the words engraved on the dial. But what could be better than a gift from a famous brand? Nowadays, brands release a variety of products under the name of the famous brand. But first and foremost, the brand should meet the expectations of the people who choose it. You don't buy adidas because it's a timeless pair of sneakers, but because you feel part of something bigger - a group of people who wear those shoes and seem to share the same values. It's not just a pair of sneakers, it's an opportunity to be in the company of famous people (at least in your mind). If you can build a successful brand around your product, its value will fade into the distance. You will be selling people a dream and belonging to a select few. And that will always come at a price.

The outcome is what matters. Liver surgery costs thousands of dollars, even if it only takes a few hours. The patient is not buying the surgeon's time or a medical service, he is buying his life. How about $40,000 for a week of training? That would be too expensive. Many people would disagree. True, it is a little cheaper than a year's tuition at any famous university in America. But this course helps millionaires become billionaires. It doesn't matter how much the product costs if it produces results that are much more expensive in the future than the price of producing and selling it.

You are not lost. You can and should have a pricing strategy. - Combine the two. In this day and age, the principle of cost plus low-cost profit will also work. For many companies, pricing is a floor they can't go below. The main point of this chapter is that an expensive product is okay. Even if it didn't cost that much to fulfill the contract, it's not that expensive or difficult. Their desire is not to work hard, but to make a lot of money.

# Chapter 4.

# Words and phrases that get in the way of selling.

Where Do Objections Come From?
Objections don't really come from nowhere; they come from you. You create these objections in the process of closing the deal. Objections come from a person's rejection of what you tell him or her in the sales process. It's the other party's rejection of what you're trying to offer. For example, suppose you offer to sign a contract. But a contract to sign does not appeal to him. An agreement between the parties sounds much better. People want to be powerful and lordly, so to speak. Not to pay, but to invest. That means to make a profit. They don't want to spend money. You might ask, "When do you want it delivered to your house? Very easy to say. It's always nice. "When do you want to give this gift to your wife? "When do you want this ring to shine on your wife's hand for hours?" It's about softening the words you use when you make a deal. Make them feel good. There just won't be any objections with that approach. Everybody wants to invest. Everybody wants to give gifts. Everybody wants the item in their home. You create all the objections by talking to people with formal words, and you create objections in people.

People want to invest, not give money. They don't want to sign contracts, they want to have an agreement. They don't want to buy, they want to have it in their home.

They want to start something to change their lives. So you have to listen to what the customer is saying. Your job is to listen to how this person wants to buy a product from you. If you remove some of the objections in the first sentences, they will buy from you. There will still be objections, but they will be few. You can write down the most common phrases on a piece of paper and change them with a positive meaning. Rephrase your responses to them. No one wants to buy. I want to invest and sign a contract. This will soften things and some objections will disappear.

Words and phrases that hinder sales.
People often use words and phrases that offend potential customers. What exactly are the phrases that take away your profits? They are really parasite words. But you can get rid of them right now.
Remember that a sales master asks questions, not bombards the customer with a lot of prepared phrases. As a result, he speaks only 20% of the time and listens the other 80%. Because he speaks less, the weight of his words is higher. As a result, the cost of error increases. This is especially important in telephone or voice communication without video. In this case, the customer can only judge you by your voice and your manner of speaking. Therefore, it is necessary to work on this.
Think about it. Now let's discuss the phonological points.
Passive voice. These are sentences in which there is no subject (acting person), but only the object of the subject of the action.

"We will deliver the goods tomorrow" is a promise of action. "Delivering the goods tomorrow" is the passive voice. Removing the subject from this sentence removes the responsibility that the customer subconsciously feels. If something goes wrong, who do you blame? However, sometimes it is necessary to remove responsibility. "After 10 days, access to discounts will be restricted." That's the offer. It was unpleasant news, but you brushed it off. Instead of accepting the decision, you said, "Okay, limited access. No big deal. That's just the way it is."

Returning verbs. This is a way to absolve yourself of responsibility. "Our product will solve your problem instantly." "So the problem will solve itself" is what the customer unconsciously hears. Why do you need your product if it's going to solve itself?

Indefinite personal sentence. An indefinite-person sentence is when the person in the sentence is not the doer of the action, but for some reason doesn't want to name the subject. This is usually because the seller thinks people will be bored with the details. "A sample contract will be emailed to you" sounds like something is being withheld. Who is sending it to you? Some people aren't sure. If you don't want to be seen as a dishonest person, be honest. "Then my assistant will email you a sample contract". Use indefinite sentences only when you want to distance yourself from what other people have said. For example, "We are told that an inflation-protected investment is a good investment. We don't think so and guarantee 15 percent a year.

Management Principles. Many salespeople believe that serious people should talk like officials. "As an official representative of Company N, we hope you will consider working with us in a number of areas. We will send you an invitation by e-mail shortly." This kind of nonsense can still be found in many texts that companies give to sales representatives. It's arrogant, boring, and highly ineffective. The more salespeople like this in a company, the less money in the business. I'm not just talking about salespeople's scripted words. The same goes for advertising slogans. Let's forget once and for all about "young and dynamic company" or "amazing quality of service". Abstract expression. What is "fast delivery"? "Highest quality." "Our service will surprise you." All of this is just information noise that doesn't help the customer in any way. Without a concrete offer, salespeople are doomed to failure. Sales champions know their product inside and out. "Engine capacity, so many cubic centimeters, to be exact - but in this case, the technical parameters do not matter. This is a Jaguar. This car is a work of art, not a number on a price tag. Please feel free to get in and drive away.

Changing a bad habit is easier than quitting smoking. And if you really want results, you can do it. Rewrite your lines from the last conversation based on the information you just learned.

You can practice in front of a mirror. And apply all this to your work.

If you're not afraid of high prices, your clients won't be either.

Now you are going to learn the most important techniques. If you don't use them, you won't sell anything. Suppose I have $100 for you, you have $100 for me. We exchange them. That doesn't look very interesting. Let's change the situation and I give you $100 and you only give me $1. That's a Klondike, that's a very good deal. You realize, of course, that this is a good idea.

In any business, in any sale, it's the value that matters, not the price. That is, what you are trying to sell should be worth more than the money the person paid for it.

Your job and your primary responsibility is to determine the value of your service or product. And to make sure that the value is greater than the price. Let's say that at the top of the list is your customer. The customer has a problem, and they have a solution, and that's your product. You have to recognize that instead of focusing on the product.

You have to focus on the customer and their problem.

If you focus on the product and not the customer and their problem, you will never understand what value the customer is looking for and what they are willing to pay for. This is a common mistake salespeople make, they start talking when they don't have the right to. If you talk more than your customers, you won't be able to sell anything. Your product or service is a great thing, but if it doesn't solve the customer's problem, the person won't buy it. If it doesn't help solve the problem, it has no value to the customer.

All thIf you know the customer's problems, then you can say that this product ticks e boxes to solve their problems.

People always have criteria. Less important and more important. If you ask a person what is important to him, he will name a quality that always has something more important behind it than the first one.

What do you need money for?

"I want to improve the situation of my family."
"What exactly do you want to improve? "I want to send my kids to a good college." "Why?"
"I want them to have a good education." "Why do they need a good education?"
"To give the child a head start in life and to get a prestigious job." "Great."
When you give a person a solution to a problem, you're giving them something more than just your product. The higher the bar, the more emotional it is. You often hear people on the other end of the phone start to cry. This is a very serious situation because we come to the criteria. You are the only person in the world who has gotten to the real reason why they need your product. You are the only one who can solve that problem. A person only wants to buy when they have a strong emotion. This is the difference between wanting to buy and needing to buy. You buy only when you want to buy. This emotion is a very powerful emotion. Focus on the customer and ask the right questions. You'll find the real problem. And like a real doctor, you get to the real cause.

Then and only then do you have the right to talk about the product.

Why does this person have this problem? And what they want to do to solve it, they have the right to talk about it. You have to understand that value should always come before price. If you don't understand that value should always come before price, then you have no right to sell. Define the true criterion, that is, the true reason, and until you find a solution in the form of a product for that customer, you have no right to talk.
Only then will he understand and buy. Because he has a better product, a better solution to his own problem.

If you're not afraid of high prices, your customers won't be either. Selling at a high price is a good thing. But you don't know how to prove it to your customers, your employees, or yourself. Let me prove it to you.

All you have to do is adopt the techniques that have made hundreds of people rich. Once you understand these sales principles, the price of the product will no longer matter. You'll be able to sell the way you want to sell.

Signs of the Right Product. Salespeople are taught that their job is to give the customer a reason to buy. That sounds logical, but it doesn't work. There are many reasons to go jogging in the morning. But you can't get kicked out for jogging. The clue is that every action has a reason, but most reasons don't lead to action. So the master salesman didn't argue. He made an offer that the customer couldn't refuse, even if they wanted to. After all, if they refused now, they would regret it later. Such win-win offers always honor the fundamental principle of selling. Value over price. But that's only one thing they have in common.

Henry Ford once said: "Thinking is the hardest job in the world. Maybe that's why so few people do it." If people have a hard time simply understanding a proposition, it won't resonate with them. People prefer things that are simple and easy to understand. Easy-to-read books are more popular than philosophical books, and comic-book movies are more popular than complex movies. So be concise and simple, use plain language, and clearly state what the customer will get as a result. It is said that a proposal should be such that even adult people can understand it. There are certain conventions. If we are talking to experts, we need to use complex terminology that they are familiar with. However, "We'll bring you goods from China in a week" is much better than "We offer a full range of transportation services. Value for twice the price, that's undeniable. However, most people will think twice before agreeing. It's probably a scam - that's the natural reaction to such an offer. Everyone subconsciously assumes that the deal must be mutually beneficial. If it's not, it's a scam. However, sometimes an offer seems incredible because it is unique. You should explain how it is possible and back up your words with testimonials from happy customers who have already purchased your product.

People act more cooperatively under tight deadlines. A famous university once conducted an experiment in which students were divided into groups and given different deadlines to complete a task. The first group was given a very short time. The second group was given twice as much time.

The third group was given no time at all. The research showed that the first group had the best results, while the third group had the highest number of people who did not complete the task at all. We know that fake timers on websites are a problem. But if customers don't feel the need to act immediately, they won't buy. People who say "I'll think about it and get back to you" often forget the urgency of the situation.

Ease of purchase. You know why TV marketers are able to sell everything in bulk. Customers make a purchase decision before they change their mind. All they have to do is dial a simple number, provide their credit card information and a shipping address. Within minutes, everything is ready to ship. This principle was transferred to the Internet. The easier it was to order goods, the more people ordered. People refused to order because they didn't want to fill out dozens of forms. Sales assistants working in high-value sales are often inseparable from paperwork. However, minimizing administrative work can be beneficial. For example, provide sample contracts so that both companies' legal departments don't have to fight over changes. Otherwise, opportunities may be missed and contracts may break down.

Minimize risk. Customers always ask, "What if they don't like the product? What if the product is not as good as described? What if it's a scam?" All of these questions are caused by the customer's uncertainty about you and about themselves. As a result, the customer perceives the purchase as a gamble. And most people subconsciously avoid risky investments.

Convince your customers that they are getting a solution to a problem, not just a sum of money. Proof, certificates, research results - in short, anything that confirms the effectiveness of the product.

A powerful step is a money-back guarantee. People get hung up on the final decision. "If I don't like it, I'll get my money back" - this idea puts the buying decision in the middle. They are more likely to make that decision. Strong desire. The salesman sees the root of the problem, he takes away your pain. But if a new model comes out with advanced features that he needs for his work, then he will definitely buy it. Because it takes away his pain and helps him increase his capabilities and therefore his profits. If the product solves their problem and helps them become a better version of themselves, people will be happy to buy it. If you prove it can do that, you don't have to sell it. The world's greatest salesman is your customer.

Does every product have to meet all of these conditions? If the goal is to get as many customers as possible, yes. But the nature of business often forces us to sift through the traffic. They say there is no such thing as a perfect tango. There are no mistakes in sales. Skilled salespeople can break the mold. As long as they know why they're doing it. Beginners, on the other hand, can simply follow directions and hone their skills. After all, skills come with experience.

It's not what you sell that buys.

Once upon a time, what you have now was beyond the reach of the common man. Only the very wealthy could afford most of the things you have now.

Before machine tools, most things were made for certain people. It was only when they began to be produced in large quantities that it became possible to buy certain things.

Why do people buy?
Let's look at why people buy things. There has always been only one reason - survival. If a person didn't have time to wear a nice dress or suit, why would he want to? People could usually only wear it in their imagination. The only reason people buy things is not because they need them, but because they want to feel them.

Imagine we're having a conversation. "Why do you want to sell more?" "Do I need it to make my business successful? To have more money."
"Why do you need more money?"
"So I can buy a bigger house." "Why do you want a bigger house?" "I want my children to have a bigger house in case something happens to me. I want to pay it off without a loan. I want my children and my family to have a place to live.

In other words. These are all feelings. And they range from the simple to the larger and more global in a person's life. They go from the trivial to the important. For the future of my children. For example, when someone wants to buy a fancy car. Why? "I want people to know that I work hard and have achieved something. Then maybe I can find someone to love me. When I was a child, I didn't have love. This means that if you sell a piece of iron in the form of a car, that is his life's dream, his dream of love.

If you sell a piece of iron in the form of a car, it probably won't bring that person any results. But if you sell it and you know why the person wants to buy it, and you give it to him, of course he will buy it. Because with this sale, you're not making a deal, you're investing in your customer's future, their better life. People always want a better life. They no longer want to survive, they want to better themselves and make their lives easier. In the time of slavery, there were slaves who survived. The time of slavery is over. Now everyone can improve their lifestyle and make their lives better. The most important thing is what they live for.

The criterion is always what is most important. And the most important thing is life, so if you dig deep enough, you will find the most important answer. What am I living for? To grow my business, to earn more, to afford more, to improve the quality of my life.

First we start with the "who," that's you. Then "how", which is how you want to make money. And how much you want. Then "what" you want to do with the money. Always starting with you, who you are, who you really are. What kind of money you want. What you want to do with it. You can read a script or you can read something on a piece of paper. If you don't change who you are, you're not going to get anything. You can go online and download sales scripts. There are thousands of scripts out there. But it's not going to change your life. To change anything, you have to change yourself.

There's no such thing as a business problem. Everything in life works or doesn't work and this applies to all aspects. Relationships, happiness, love, and most importantly, money. If you can make money, you don't need a script on paper. Not a script, but you have to change yourself. To change yourself, you have to reprogram the old program. The wrong program. You have to reprogram yourself.

I want to help you raise the bar of your life one step at a time. First you make $1,000, then $2,000. Then three, four, five, six, seven, ten, twenty, thirty... and then you make a million. You will never jump over yourself and your development. Why not? Because as soon as you jump over, you start stumbling. And that's when life punishes you. It brings you back to the place you missed. The longer you resist and the longer you believe that self-proclaimed business coaches with a microphone. The more you believe them, the more miserable and poor you'll be. This book is meant to give each of you a chance to become successful and rich, to show you the way. It's up to you. Nobody can help you. Because if you don't want to live this life, nobody will help you.

Why do people buy? How can you sell if you don't understand what really influences your customer? We uncover the true context of every sale and help you understand the context of every transaction at a deep level. What is your goal? How much time do you have to get there? What barriers are holding you back?

Emotional Selling: How Emotions Work. We have long lived in the age of brands.

Instead of buying a product, we buy the emotions that come from belonging to something great and belonging to a group. So if you're currently selling technology, products or services, get ready to kiss your business goodbye. Or start putting what you've learned into practice.

The heart rules. You may think of yourself as an extremely rational person, but you are wrong. After all, making decisions with your head is the most practical task that requires you to mobilize your mental resources. Thinking with the heart is different. We see, hear, and feel everything going on around us and act on our intuition. These impulses are not always right, but they are the most sincere. In other words, engaging the emotional side is far more important than engaging the rational side. As millions of people around the world know, Apple suggests a different way of thinking. Red Bull is invigorating. Driving a Toyota is a dream. Owning a MasterCard is convenient the world over. Because these brands spend a lot of money, time and effort to win the hearts and minds of the masses. It's not just a slogan. Brands are a way to unite people who may seem to have little in common. And the emotional benefits can outweigh the functional drawbacks. When the first generation of iPhones came out, no one cared that they couldn't set their own ringtones. Millions of people use Instagram, but they didn't complain that they couldn't post even simple links. When a Range Rover breaks down, the body has to be removed from the frame, but fans of premium SUVs aren't the least bit affected. If you give consumers the right emotional connection, they won't look for flaws.

This is the goal of emotional branding. It's much easier to influence emotions when you know exactly which emotional line to touch. Imagine that you are not only selling a product, but also an emotion. In most cases, your customers will fall into at least one of the following buyer types.

Poor. No, that doesn't mean they're strapped for cash. It means that such a customer really needs your product. Saying "I'm just thinking about it" or "I'll buy it in a year or two" is not enough. They need a firm conviction, and that's what should set the tone for your actions. Be specific and clear, and show that you are willing to solve the problem. Of course, none of this is an excuse to be pushy.

Conservative. Unlikely to be receptive to innovative ideas. This type of customer will usually pay for something they already know, or at least something similar to a familiar brand. Offering a standard product at a moderate price is sufficient for this type of customer. To stand out, emphasize reliability and practicality, and add an element of nostalgia. Things like "childhood memories" are for conservatives.

A dignified, successful and wealthy person chooses goods and services with status in mind. He is even willing to pay a higher price for appropriate quality and the opportunity to show his status. Any price can attract such a buyer if it reflects the right value. In other words, everything must be perfect.

Hippies. They do not like recommendations and have a clear disdain for mass-produced goods. These are usually young people for whom their own feelings are more important than other people's opinions.

Yes, they may buy a motorcycle for freedom, but sometimes a skateboard is enough.

Nevertheless, it is not difficult to anticipate their impulsive purchases. Your products and services should reflect their personality.

Pleasure Seekers. Just getting "pleasure" is valued above all else. Restrictions cause them considerable discomfort and they do not want to deny themselves. In addition, such a buyer will not bargain if the thing he really likes. The hedonist believes that the ideal life is a series of vacations. Therefore, give him the right feelings. Everything should be simple and fun.

Imitator. He does not have his own desires and point of view. This person simply imitates what he sees on the TV screen or in advertisements. He takes examples from various authority figures, dresses well, goes on diets and loses weight, buys gadgets and spends money. There are two ways to beat the copycat: The first is to keep an eye on new products and respond quickly to those that are relevant to your niche. The second is to use your personality to project authority. Because he likes to hear what others have to say.

Newcomer. This type of customer rarely focuses on high-end products and services because they are young and have few economic opportunities. However, they also like to stand out and rely on the novelty of their ideas. It is important for them to be among the first, even if they later realize that the purchase is not so necessary. Newcomers will help you a lot in the beginning. If you create an atmosphere of exclusivity and novelty, the product of the future.

Emotions allow you to offer maximum value at minimum cost. Everything must become a brand. Your product, your company, and you. Go beyond the cost + markup formula to offer more to your customers and get more in return. Thousands of brands and millions of fans prove it.

## Chapter 5.

## The Biggest Obstacles in Sales.

When you think of a salesperson, what comes to mind is. Who are salespeople? They are speculators, crafty people who only see money. All they want to do is sell you a product. They just want your money. My parents used to tell me this. If you don't study, you don't have a future. A boy comes home from school. And he says, "I had this class where they asked everybody what they wanted to be. "Some people said they wanted to be a doctor, an engineer. I decided to be a salesman. "How did you come to that? I teach you, I educate you, I feed you, and you. It's terrible. God is punishing me. Why is this happening? Why is it that when you try to sell something to somebody, your palms start sweating and your heart jumps out of your chest? Because you've been taught since childhood that the most dangerous people are strangers. Why can't you talk to them? Because you've been taught that it's scary to talk to someone on the phone, but they won't hurt you. But for some reason you're afraid to say your name, to show your face. It's like you're going to be chased and robbed or even killed. I don't want to hang out with horrible people. I don't want to deal with all that.

It's a phobia. And how do you think you're going to fight that? Let's look at where sales come from. When you talk to people you don't know. People you know will never buy from you.

In other words, your profits are directly proportional to the number of strangers you talk to. To keep your subconscious mind from getting dirty, you're forbidden to do the only thing in the world that can make you money. Don't think that speculators are thieves. Entrepreneurs are the worst. We go to the shops and the prices are too high. Everything should be sold at cost. They should be forced to work for free.

People who say such things are poor people. This means that the program that governs your whole life comes from poverty. Only a beggar doesn't realize that.

All the money you get belongs to someone else. You don't know that person. To get that money, you have to talk to a complete stranger. You control every aspect of your life. No matter how hard you try, no matter how motivated you are. How you find out who you are and what programs are built into you. It's what results you get. What kind of fruit grows on a tree is what kind of roots it has. If there are apples on that tree. The roots of that tree are also apples. The roots of an orange tree, so oranges grow, all right, the logic is there. The fact that you're not making money is all in your subconscious mind. Your subconscious mind controls everything in your life. Even the way you blink, the way you breathe. Your subconscious controls you. How are you going to spend your life? What state of mind are you going to be in? Whether you will be in luxury or poverty is controlled by your subconscious mind. So if there are roots of poverty in your subconscious mind, you will get the same result. People don't change.

So if you are constantly stressed. If you are always short of money, the root of that comes from poverty.

All you have to do is change your subconscious. Our job is to change your subconscious. You can be proud of what you do. If you're in sales, don't be afraid of your customers. Be confident in yourself. And you are not a speculator and you are not a cheat.

You make people happy, you solve their problems. And they will be happy to pay you. Only then can your business be successful.

Sales is one of the three components of your business. How the business works. The first is customer acquisition. The whole world is already on the Internet. That's how you get customers.

The second is selling only what people want and need. The third step is customer service.

In other words. It all starts with attracting people, but oddly enough, you can't attract people until you learn how to sell. That is why most businesses fail. If you want to know how to solve this problem, unravel it, straighten it, align it. Clear your subconscious mind and you will restart your life and your business. Most people have failed at more than one business. Why is that? It doesn't matter what technique you use, it doesn't matter what script you read. It doesn't matter what product you make. If you hate yourself and what you are selling. So most likely you have to decide if there is a problem. Analyze that problem. If there is poverty, then the roots are the same. If you change your roots then your business and your whole life will change.

The biggest obstacles in selling. There is something preventing you from becoming a successful salesperson. It is inside you and it is actively destroying you. The result is self-sabotage, why is this happening? You need to dig into your memory and find the events that are sabotaging your sales mindset. Becoming your new self is not easy.

Stereotypes get in the way of selling.
You are not alone in letting past experiences shape your perception of selling. Some information stored in everyone's memory has led millions of salespeople to misinterpret situations and follow failed programs. Here are three stereotypes that are long overdue.
The customer is always right. Let's put aside for the moment the waiter who expects a generous tip and whose boss makes him flatter even the most obnoxious customers. Sure, sometimes this approach works, but overall it's a losing battle. For you and, oddly enough, for the customer. Believe me, if you only work on the client's terms, you will never be satisfied with the money you get. Endless changes, unfair discounts, a lot of unnecessary effort - the result is the same. Is this really necessary? Isn't it better to let the problem customers go and work with the right ones?
It's also undesirable to be too flexible with the customer. After all, who else but you can tell them to do what you say without making a single change to the project? Otherwise, you will have to prove that cheap does not mean good and that you should choose expensive products. Without expert advice, the buyer will make the wrong choice.

Despite your best efforts to please him, he will blame you.

The customer always understands nothing about my product. This stereotype is very different from the previous one. In fact, this stereotype may cause buyers to overlook you. Those who like to indulge their ego may prefer this option. However, from a business standpoint, this approach is difficult. There are several reasons for this. First, no matter how hard you try to hide this attitude, it sometimes comes out. It is enough to say something in an irritated or condescending tone, and the client will understand everything and decide not to deal with you anymore. Even if your interlocutor is the smartest person on the planet, he will not listen to you. Second, you run the risk of putting yourself in a stupid situation. You may have heard the story of the microwave salesman who showed an elderly man a fan and tried to explain how it worked. The poor salesman didn't realize that his customer was a radiophysicist and ended up looking like an idiot. I won't even try to explain how blatantly deceptive you are. Yet you continue to lie and desperately try to steer your customers in the direction you want them to go. The next fool, however, may not be so easy. Worst of all, that person will go public. Loyal customers are the key to stability. In an ideal world, the situation looks like this. Customers see your ads, are happy with the quality of your products and the level of your service, and order regularly for years to come, ensuring a steady profit. After all, it's easier and less stressful. However, not all repeat customers are equally useful. Analysis shows that many bring a very small and narrow order.

If a new client came to you with such an order, you would probably not take it, but you do because it is inconvenient to refuse the "old guys". Sometimes you even lose money. Besides, in a way, a constant circle of clients keeps you in one place. You become grateful to them for this "stability" and do not try to explore new territories. After all, it is more convenient and easier to work this way. On the other hand, clients who are willing to pay more and enjoy working with you will pay others. You end up limiting your opportunities. Of course, this is no reason to downplay the value of a primary partner. What's important is that the value of that advantage doesn't prevent you from seeing new potential clients.

Customers come in all shapes and sizes, and it is the Sales Assistant's job to find the right strategy for each customer from the variety of tools available. However, replacing tools with templates or reducing their number can lead to job termination. If the salesperson doesn't break this stereotype soon, he or she will be out of a job.

Ways to use reverse psychology in sales.
Let's talk about the right way to make cold calls. Because in the age of the Internet, applications already come from there. But still, if you come across a company that doesn't know or even have an idea how to do it. They don't know that there is marketing that deals with customer acquisition and you are forced to make cold calls. Let's think about how to make it better, more interesting and more profitable.

So there is this technique. When you get a call from a company trying to sell you something, how do you recognize it? A cold call is when a person talks fast and tries to tell you everything in seconds before you hang up. But in real life, it's the opposite. When you change your tactics. "You called me and asked me to call you back, and I'll do that. Did you have something to offer me?" Then it sounds completely different, breaks the pattern. Let's say an assistant picks up the phone. You say that his boss called you. "Why, did he want to offer me something? The secretary told me and left a note with this number on it. I want to know why?" Where do you think they're more likely to be contacted? Where there's a better chance of hooking a person and getting them interested. You can use that technique.

 Isn't it always more profitable to talk to people who come to your site? They've learned what you sell, answered a few questions, chosen your product and are waiting for your call. I'd like to remind you again that the most important thing in business is to get customers. If the owner of this business is negligent, why would you sell in his business? Chances are that the business is based on misconceptions. That means the person has come up with nonsense that no one wants and has people with no sales experience calling and going into people's homes and selling them something they don't need.

 But if people are looking for this product. Their family's future depends on it, solves long-standing problems, do you think it's an easy sell? I mean, if you sell something useful and you don't force it on people.

So the first thing you have to do is find a product that solves a serious problem for a person. And the more serious the problem that the product, good or service solves, the easier it is to sell, the more applications. It's foolish to sell something people don't know about something they don't need.

Stop selling what nobody needs. Get some experience. And then go out and sell what they need.

The Best Cold Calling Scripts. Using reverse psychology techniques, you can take the stress out of your first call and get a prospect to open up to your offer. Now you know how to play the "reverse game" correctly. This will get the client to make excuses for your call. Try this method! Also, use digital marketing and you can forget about cold calling forever.

How to use reverse psychology in sales.

Marketing textbooks say that "reverse" selling was first discovered by David Sandler in 1967. That's ridiculous! Tom Sawyer pioneered the approach. To avoid painting the fence white, he convinced his colleagues that there was no better profession. His co-workers believed him and even paid him in small change for the opportunity to paint. Tom Sawyer is clearly a master salesman. You've learned how to make excuses for calls to get your customers to make excuses. Of course, this isn't the only way to use reverse psychology in sales. There are other super effective ways. "Would you please rate this offer on a scale of one to ten?"

Ask this when you've told the customer enough and they're still hesitating. And you'll often get a 6 or 7. They'll be genuinely surprised: "I didn't think I could get more than a 4. And I got a 7?" After saying these words, the customer, who was just waiting for the dialog to end, will start listing the benefits of your offer. And if you just let him talk, he'll mentally add a few points to his original estimate. Sometimes that's enough to get them to buy. But you can go a step further. You can start questioning the benefits he lists: "Plus, fast shipping. If I accept, you promised I'd get it the day after tomorrow." "What's the big deal? Any company can deliver to you the same day." "No, you know what? I recently ordered another item and the delivery was just terrible. I was promised it would be delivered in one day, but instead I got a week's worth of breakfast." "That's disgusting. No, we don't have that kind of rude behavior here.

Another way is, "I don't think you can afford it. Everyone has been a victim of this technique at least once in their life. But because it is so deeply ingrained in the human psyche, it almost never fails. Let's say you pick out a business suit, and the salesman-consultant circles around you: "Look at this one. Or this one I think will suit you. Put that one aside, it's too expensive...". "What do you mean, expensive? How much? 1000 $. Don't I look like a man who can afford $1000 suits?" "I'm sorry, I don't mean to be rude, but I thought you might want to buy something cheaper." "Let me see. I'll put it on now." Much of the effectiveness of this technique has nothing to do with the product. Whether it's sneakers, dinner at a restaurant, or a multi-million dollar castle.

This technique can be combined with rule breaking. The customer thinks the salesman will never wake up to say that his product is overpriced. He must insist that the value is much greater than the price. "How much? 500 $. The first appointment is for $500?" "Yes, that's right. That's a lot of money for you, isn't it? Can you really afford it?" "It's not about the money! If, as you say, it really works."

A very effective method. "Can you make this decision for yourself?" Clients love to hear advice, especially when it comes to big deals. They just don't want to make a rash decision and not be able to say so directly. And wanting to discuss the offer with someone is a good reason to delay. You have the opportunity to use this trump card at the beginning of the interview. "Before I begin, I'd like to clarify a few points." "Yes, I'm listening." "Do you have the authority to make a decision, or do you need to consult someone else? Don't get me wrong, this offer is limited. We can't afford to wait. If you need advice, that's fine. Maybe our offer isn't for you." "Of course I make my own decisions! In fact, I'm the only boss in the company. Show me everything."

Isn't it only when we are young that we act on instinct? The spoiled child lives in everyone at every age. It's a character trait, because we want to be independent. We don't like to do what we are told, we don't like to be judged by others, and we don't like to give in to the pleas of salespeople. A master salesperson understands this and often uses reverse psychology. "Don't use these techniques in your work! It's only for real professionals."

# Chapter 6.

## The Most Common Mistake Salespeople Make.

Salespeople talk a lot about big opportunities, show numbers, and threaten deadlines. But it won't work if you have all kinds of junk in your head. People who are looking for freebies or who are afraid of money will meet losers along the way. In the end, people sell exactly what they buy. That's how the "law of attraction" you read about in fancy books really works.

Psychological Signs of Poverty. If you're reading this book, it's relevant to you. If not, you are probably vacationing on a yacht right now, thinking about where to invest your free money. It's time to admit how bad things are. After all, the first step to recovery is recognizing the seriousness of the problem.

Here are some of them:
Blaming others for the problems in your life. Usually with good reason. No one ever taught your father or mother to be parents to emulate. Many people simply grew up in same-sex families. Almost everyone has experienced heartache. Everyone, without exception, has had to deal with tyrannical bosses, relatives who were a bad influence, acquaintances, and co-workers. Yes, nothing disappears without a trace. But it is up to you whether these scars will destroy your future. Now imagine the person responsible for your pain and point your finger at him or her: "It's all your fault."

There is only one finger pointing at him and three fingers pointing at you. You are holding on to your comfort zone. Even if it's uncomfortable. You agree to work for pennies on the dollar with the guarantee that you will do so until you die. "At least there's stability." - You tell yourself that because you're afraid it's going to get worse, and you're faking it, but you're really afraid of change, of uncertainty, of reality. You know where stability is. It's in the morgue and the cemetery. Until you get there, enjoy the unknown. Don't give up your ambitions.

You know everything. How to fix the plumbing, how to raise a child, how to start a business, how to invest, and the meaning of life. An online course is a relatively honest way to make money. Business books. Are worthless. Mentors. What can they teach you that you don't already know? But here's the thing: "You don't know." "Know-it-alls don't get reviewed in Forbes, they work in taxis. If you're so smart, why are you so poor? Ask yourself.

Fear of failure. "What if it doesn't work? - comes into your mind every time and you are inactive. It's very simple. If you are afraid of being considered stupid and incompetent, you will remain stupid and incompetent. Dumb people only learn from their mistakes. Wise people come to teachers. But both are destined to make mistakes. Success is achieved only by those who come out of failure without losing enthusiasm.

Hate those who succeed. You have no doubt that the young man who drives the fancy car is the son of a bum, that the woman is of easy conduct, that the billionaires are

involved in corruption in government contracts, and that those who have nothing to show for it are probably very bad people. How can you get rich if you don't believe that the path to great wealth inevitably involves crime, connections, and moral filth? Rely on reliable information. This applies not only to those who jump to conclusions about others, but also to the business world. Leave the discussions to the grandmothers at the door.

Rely on the opinions of others. Rely on the opinions of family, friends, colleagues, and acquaintances. The more people whose opinions matter to you, the harder it will be to get out of your rut. Angry comments and "dislikes" from strangers are enough to discourage you. If you can't get ahead in your career without these signs of approval, I've got bad news for you. "What will people think?" you say. Calm down. People don't care. Not about you, not about each other. They have their own concerns.

You justify yourself. You should have been successful a long time ago, but you didn't have the time. You should have started a business a long time ago, but you're having trouble understanding the intricacies of the law. You want to build a website, but you're not a programmer. I believe that the accumulation of excuses leads to poverty - it's an undeniable fact. Instead of making dozens of excuses, find at least one opportunity. Then start taking action, even if it's difficult and time-consuming.

The middleman comes first. You think it is shameful to spend your hard-earned money on yourself. First you must provide for your family and friends.

Then, when the time comes that everyone is happy (which is unlikely because it will only increase the need), you will start giving to animal shelters. This is the "debt" that ruins your life. You always feel indebted to your parents, your children, your relatives and your country. And your own desires are always left behind. Take care of yourself. Elvis Presley bought several pink Cadillacs and only then gave one to his mother. Warren Buffett became the greatest philanthropist of our time after becoming one of the richest people in the world.

Humility. We think of it as a virtue. However, you prefer to stay in the shadows, refrain from praising yourself, and downplay your virtues. In this case, your chances of success are very slim. You have no room for humility. Only the successful rich have this luxury. And for the poor, self-confidence is not a secondary happiness, but the first and only one.

Only I will do well. Separation of duties can destroy a company. Especially in the early stages, when you have neither the money to hire a real professional nor the experience to raise a young underdog. If you want to do it right, do it yourself. This principle may help in the beginning, but eventually you'll have to give it up. Otherwise, the business will stagnate. There are no lone millionaires.

Behind every great business is a great team. You will not be able to build such a team if you do not know how to delegate.

Do any of these apply to you? If one to three apply to you, congratulations on your chances of getting out of poverty.

If four to six of these items apply to you, you need professional help. If more, you need a complete reconfiguration of your subconscious.

Using Pain to Make Sales.

Now let's talk about techniques for closing deals that don't involve a return on investment. It's very important to recognize that there is a return on investment. If you invest this much, you will get this much. There's also a technique of showing them how much they're going to lose if they don't buy a certain product. But if you tell people to invest in sales training. You can double your sales and make a lot of money. It's just a future that people don't feel. There are no guarantees. But it's called lost opportunity. It's a fact and it's already happening, it doesn't need to be proven.

Now imagine the following situation, you start with the pain that's already there, and so you make a deal that tells you how to get that investment back. You learn how to sell twice as much and double your profits. And you want to make more money. Because you need to buy a multi-million dollar house. It's been on your bucket list for a long time. The only reason you start a business is to make money and to make a profit. And you have a chance to become rich. Isn't that the right thing to do? You do everything you can to make your business grow. That's why we do what we do. That's why we reboot everybody's subconscious. You will be healthy people who want wealth, prosperity. Improve your life and your family's life.

Use pain in selling. Salesmen mostly talk about opportunity.

It all begins with return on investment. In other words, if a prospect buys a product or service now, how much profit will they make in the future? Calculate how much your sales problems are already costing you.

Try answering the following questions: Describe the customers who should be interested in your product. List at least three ways you can tell them how much revenue they are losing by not doing business with you. Review your sales force. How many of them enjoy their jobs and are they missing opportunities to develop their skills?

## Chapter 7.

## We make our own rules for talking to customers.

Let's talk about rules for communicating with customers. Many salespeople don't set any rules before they start communicating with customers. If you don't, you'll get a lot of unreasonable responses and objections. If you want to avoid such objections, start the conversation with an agenda: Before you start presenting the product, say to the interviewer: "Listen, my friend.
At the end of our conversation, I'm going to ask you one question. And you can only give me two answers. "Yes, this is what I need. Or, "No, it's not right for me. You can't hurt me with a negative answer. Our job is to find out if my services, my product is right for you.

And what happens at that point: You've already agreed from the beginning that nobody wants to hurt anybody. And he can relax and listen to what you have to say about your product during the sales process. You will calmly ask all your questions. Before you do, you can also ask him: "Before we get to the product, let me ask you a few questions to better understand if my product will meet your needs. If you have any questions, ask me. I'll answer them. And after our conversation, you'll give me a yes or no answer.
After this agenda of conversation, the transaction will be relaxed and enjoyable for both parties.

Establishing the rules of the game from the beginning and letting the other person know that you're prepared to be rejected is one of the most powerful techniques of a master salesperson. It removes the tension and makes the conversation more meaningful. When you are ready to accept rejection, the number of rejections is greatly reduced.

All prospects are like young girls. A "no" answer is likely to hide a "yes, but later" or "convince me". However, "no" may be the final answer. The skill of the salesperson is to screen out the types of rejections rather than wasting time talking to people who will never buy. To do that, you need to know why they won't buy, even if you've done everything right. Or almost everything right.

Lack of demand. You can't sell sand in the desert. People may not have a need for your product, and your benefits don't affect them in any way. They are not rational or emotional. They are not your target customers. But the problem is something else entirely. It may be the wrong place or the wrong time. Let's say you're in a hurry to get on a plane. Your hands are full, you're pressed for time, and more importantly, you don't know where to go. A cheerful guy jumps up and says, "You like pizza, don't you?" He offers you a discount. In another situation, you might have been interested in his offer. But right now you're not interested in pizza. At best, you will refuse and not even stop. If you're in a bad mood, you might even be rude. What's the problem here? You love Italian food and often order takeout. But the delivery person doesn't take the situation into account. Do we always have the thought in our head, "We should take care of this, but it's not urgent"?

That's how we're wired. In addition, we subconsciously perceive hasty decisions as frivolous. In other words, it's human nature to object to the salesperson. "Call back later" is not always a way of saying no. Maybe this customer wants to think carefully about what he's heard, has discussed it with his wife, and wants to close the deal. But problems at work, kids' mischief, and sick parents have distracted his thoughts. And the conversation began to fade from his memory. Most goods and services have no objective urgency. But you can create urgency by limiting time or quantity. "Call us now and we'll give you a discount." - There's a reason TV marketers use this approach so often; use it.

It doesn't create desire. Do you make all your purchases out of necessity? We have long been driven not by the functionality of a product, but by the overall perception of the people who use it. That's what branding is all about. Today, people don't just buy a product or service, they buy their "best self. And a master salesperson should take advantage of that. A professional should not only hit the pain points and emphasize the solution to problems, but also create a positive emotion. "I didn't just want to buy a yacht, I wanted to buy a ticket to the club of the most successful people in the world. The customer may say "no" because he doesn't understand how your product can help him get closer to his best self. So let's explain it.

I don't have enough money. If they are clearly saying, "I can't afford it," why not do the best you can for them?

Instead of giving them a discount, offer to pay in installments. However, when you hear the words, "It's too expensive for me," it's often not about the money. In the customer's eyes, the price is lower than the value. Your job is to get them to change their mind. They can't turn down an offer from a master salesperson because our customers have been convinced that value is much higher than price. They are unlikely to turn down the opportunity. When you make an offer based on this principle, you are less likely to face the objection, "I don't have that kind of money right now.

You are not trusted. People are suspicious of anyone trying to sell them something. Especially if the salesperson speaks in memorized phrases and silly words. "Greetings. The weather is sunny. Do you know how you can keep the sunny weather in your life? Put all your money in our bank, of course. And you'll get 15% interest. And you'll save it from inflation." Hearing such words, a person in his imagination draws pictures with an idiot on the other end of the wire. And rightly so. Do your best to convince them that the company you work for is truly trustworthy. Demonstrations, case studies and references, but most of all - confidence, poise, the ability to ask the right questions at the right time, and the ability to listen.

Sometimes customers don't trust themselves. For example, when offered a diet that works, they may say, "If it's not a magic pill, I'll have to run in the morning. I'll fail as usual and mess it up." "You just have to follow the instructions and follow the product recommendations." Make your offer more perfect.

Minimize the reasons and opportunities for prospects to reject you. When you do, your conversion rate will increase dramatically. This is guaranteed.

You don't have to convince the customer.

The most important advantage you have over your customer is information. It's the most important and the most powerful. Why customers come to you. He wants to solve his problem. First and foremost, you need to know what their problem is. Whether you have to give a presentation, tell a story, show a demonstration. Let's say there's a scale from 0 to 10, where 5 is the middle. And you are the one who decides where to go. If you hear in the middle of a conversation, "I don't know, maybe later. You should not waste your time with that person. In this case, use reverse psychology. In other words, tell him, "I don't think he's the right person for you, and make the client prove that he really needs him. There is a gambler's gamble in the human mentality and you have to take that into account. You have to reassess what stage your client's desire is at. And only when it is close to 8-10 can you talk about the product. How it solves a problem, how it can help in specific cases. Your job is to get the person to sell it to themselves. If the pain is not enough, no one will pay anything. The person pays to solve the pain problem.

Most people run away from pain. They don't do anything, they don't buy anything. So if you really want to sell something, you have to have a product that solves that problem. The first thing you have to do is bring the person into the pain.

He's been lying to himself for a long time, his life is falling apart. He's living in poverty, his business is failing. His friends do not associate with him and he is depressed all the time. All this needs to be exposed and shown where he stands. Many people live like this. They think everything is okay. Why is that? Because he's been told from the stage, "You can do anything you want and you have a chance no matter how old you are. Your job is to release the fear that this man has had for a long time. Then you can make the sale. That is when you will become a successful salesman and people will demand that you take their money. Then you will be able to close the deal.

You don't have to use any clever tricks to close the deal. You will not sell to anyone or anything unless the person has a pain and a need for your product. They don't need to buy what you have. This is unfortunately true, but also fortunately true. People should only buy what is truly useful, truly effective, and leads to the desired result.

End the conversation on time. Signs that your customer is ready to buy. Many deals fail because salespeople talk a lot and don't know how to listen. And they keep talking, even when the customer is ready to pay. As a result, the customer gets tired of the information and decides to come back later. It's simple. We all love to buy, but we can't stand being "shoved" in the face. That's why it's so important to know when to stop. Signs it's time to stop talking.

The customer is napping. Video calls are always better than voice calls, you have more opportunities to express yourself and the other person has less chance to cheat.

If he nods as he listens to you, that's enough. Internally, he's accepted your offer, and all that's left is to complete the formalities. "Shall we proceed to sign the contract?" In most cases, the client will say yes. If not, it is up to you to steer the conversation in the right direction. The customer's questions should clear up any remaining ambiguities.

The customer thinks more deeply about the product. Face-to-face communication opens up more possibilities. If you are selling something tangible, not a service, and the customer does not want to get away from it, it is another sign that he is ready. Without realizing it, the customer already owns it, in his mind. If the customer touches the product you just showed him, it doesn't mean anything. But if he picks it up again after a while, it means he has already made up his mind. And it's time to pay.

Shoppers pull out their wallets. Touching the wallet says nothing about its contents, and cash is quickly out of use. But habit is stronger than rational argument. When shoppers want to make a purchase, they unconsciously touch their pockets, wallets or pull out their cell phones. Even if it's a large sum of money that no one would carry.

Shoppers ask clarifying questions. "How much horsepower is that? "This is a first-level question. It doesn't mean the customer is ready to buy. He may be interested and just ask. "How fast can you get the paperwork done? - This is another level. The person asking this question has already decided what they want to buy and is trying to figure out if it will affect their plans.

If he nods as he listens to you, that's enough. Internally, he's accepted your offer, and all that's left is to complete the formalities. "Shall we proceed to sign the contract?" In most cases, the client will say yes. If not, it is up to you to steer the conversation in the right direction. The customer's questions should clear up any remaining ambiguities.

The customer thinks more deeply about the product. Face-to-face communication opens up more possibilities. If you are selling something tangible, not a service, and the customer does not want to get away from it, it is another sign that he is ready. Without realizing it, the customer already owns it, in his mind. If the customer touches the product you just showed him, it doesn't mean anything. But if he picks it up again after a while, it means he has already made up his mind. And it's time to pay.

Shoppers pull out their wallets. Touching the wallet says nothing about its contents, and cash is quickly out of use. But habit is stronger than rational argument. When shoppers want to make a purchase, they unconsciously touch their pockets, wallets or pull out their cell phones. Even if it's a large sum of money that no one would carry.

Shoppers ask clarifying questions. "How much horsepower is that?" This is a first-level question. It doesn't mean the customer is ready to buy. He may be interested and just ask. "How fast can you get the paperwork done? - This is another level. The person asking this question has already decided what they want to buy and is trying to figure out if it will affect their plans.

The customer has to convince himself that he wants and needs the product. By watching and listening to the customer, he knows when it's time to close the deal. Without wasting each other's valuable time.

## Chapter 8.

## Big Money Comes Faster.

Let's talk about the fastest and most effective way to become a master salesman. A salesman who makes a lot more money. First, let's break down the following facts. A certain percentage of entrepreneurs who stay in business will eventually make $1 million in their lifetime. The question is how to actually make $1 million as quickly as possible. Some people can make it in a year, some in a month, some in a day. But how much time are you willing to spend to make $1 million?

This is especially true for entrepreneurs. They are used to scamming and living on display. They rent an office, go into debt, put up their house as collateral. They had problems from the beginning, they had to learn how to sell. Business and making money is a sport. It takes skill and experience. No matter how much you believe in success and motivation. You may believe that you can do anything. But you still need to find someone to teach you not to make mistakes. You need to find someone like a coach. There are actually pitfalls in business that no one will tell you about. But first you have to find out who you are, who you are inside, and what is inside you that is stopping you from growing? Your job is to get the money you want in a short time, not to stretch it out for years. Efficiently and clearly. Then you can rest. Either you live in the office or you close the office. So your job is to make sure you live in the islands. Your job is to find out what you are missing and learn it.

So you're not always banging your head against the same wall when you can open the door and walk through? Is it possible to make more money in less time? The life of a salesperson is full of challenges and financial problems. So how do you achieve big goals in the shortest time possible? To achieve your goals faster, you need to shift your mindset to a different wavelength. First, answer a few questions about yourself.

What do you think about money? Surely there are people you care about. You love them and want to be there for them. Let's say you say these words to them every day. "You make me miserable. "You mean nothing to me. "I'm less of a burden without you." "You're just a means to an end." If you said that to every woman you met, how likely would it be that you would end up alone? It's obvious. How can you get rich if you keep repeating these phrases about money? Yes, paper money is not the same as a living person. But it's a matter of attitude and behavior. It's very simple. People who despise money cannot get rich.

Would you want a large amount of money for doing nothing? Let's say you have a small amount of dollars deposited into your account every 24 hours. You can spend it on whatever you want, but you can't withdraw cash. At the end of the day, whatever's left will burn up. And there is no guarantee that this unprecedented amount of money will be available tomorrow. What would you do in such a situation? You would definitely spend it all until the end. You would spend all the money every day. Or maybe I'm wrong. You know where these dollars come from.

They are your minutes of life. And whether you use them wisely or not, they burn up. Who knows if you'll have a tomorrow. Why waste precious minutes every day instead of seizing opportunities?
 Why do you need a lot of money? Most people will say, "I want to be rich. You will probably answer the same way. Usually people get stuck on this question because they don't know how to set goals. Without clear goals, you cannot make a clear plan of action. What does it mean to be "rich"? And "success". These beautiful words are used in place of goals, but they don't help. Goals must be specific. "I want to earn $20,000 a month." But at the same time, goals should not be overly ambitious. Sitting in a small, cheap apartment and trying to get on the list of billionaires is ridiculous. That is for real connoisseurs of big capital. Finally, the goal must also be a great passion. This is the most powerful engine of successful people, next to cold calculation. In the end, you may not get where you want to go, but you will feel fulfilled. Life is unpredictable and circumstances often change our goals.
 If you found yourself in a foreign country with two hundred dollars, what would you do? Most likely, you would rent a penniless shack and get a lousy job. After all, you have to survive. Or you could invest all your money in an expensive suit and a membership in an elite club. That's what one young immigrant did. A few years later, he was a millionaire. Maybe this story is a bit exaggerated, but it illustrates the possibilities and the attitude towards oneself.

Usually your income is the income of your family of five. And the desired limit of your family income is the amount in your boss's paycheck. Yes, they say that students who can't outperform their mentors are bad students. But in reality, very few do. To earn at least twice your current income, you must first get out of your beggarly environment and find a mentor who will make you realize that this amount of money is insignificant. As long as you think like a beggar and look like a beggar, you will never get rich.

If you have read this book carefully, you have learned a lot. But this book will not help you if you do not take action now. Write down the conclusions you have drawn for yourself and the actions you will take. Remember, the journey always begins with the first step.

Tips for Using Notepads in Sales.

A famous man was a really rich man. He bought an office in the Trump Building for two million dollars. This businessman stayed there on very rare occasions to look at the sea from the top of the fiftieth floor. Actors and celebrities sometimes stayed there. These meetings were always very funny and rewarding. What surprised me the most was that he wrote down everything important to him in his notebook. I would like to show you this technique of working with a notebook. Why is it important to write down what the client says? Because it makes the client feel important. You are the one who takes everything this person says seriously. When you're selling over the phone with a video call, your job is not to type. It's to put pen to paper.

You can ask beforehand, "Can I take notes? This is very important. I need to fully understand your situation. So I can find the best way to help you. For example. Ask where he/she would like to have a home. What is important to the person? Availability of a shopping center, ocean view, etc. Be sure to write this down. Once you have everything written down, simply ask the person, "Based on what I have written down, you want so-and-so. Am I getting this right? Is this what you're looking for?" If you meet the client's needs based on the notes, they'll be happy. Even if he knows the technique. He'll still enjoy talking to someone who takes notes and really appreciates every word his client says. We all want to be heard. To be understood, not confused. It's a very powerful technique. And when you find a solution, you say, "This is exactly what you're looking for. "Overlooking the sea, a shop 300 meters away, and this and that are close. Everything you asked for, I've written it down. I think it's perfect for you. Congratulations, all that's left is for you to sign our contract. When would you like to move in?" People don't want what's for sale. They want something different, they want their dreams to come true. And you can make that happen. Listen, take notes, show that you care, show that you understand what is important to the customer. Find just the right option and solve the problem. Effective ways to think differently.

Empathy - Empathy, the salesperson's weapon of choice. Instead of being seen as a pushy salesperson trying to pick your pocket, you need to be seen as someone who understands and wants to help.

There are simple ways to be just that person.
Put yourself in the customer's shoes. The customer resists and fights back. A master salesperson can fend them off by asking precise questions. This is especially true when explaining why you shouldn't let the customer take the lead. After all, boldness and confidence are far more useful than timidity. But selling isn't a battle between the customer and the salesperson. It is a confrontation between the customer and his problem. The job of the master salesperson is to convince the customer that we are on the same side. But first we must define the problem. People don't like to talk to strangers about their problems. Especially if it hurts their self-esteem. The boss was embarrassed that his attempt to delegate some of the work to a deputy had failed. After all, he chose the deputy who turned out to be incompetent. Might he have similar concerns about salespeople who are networkers? And how will he deal with those who talk down to him? Empathy is not sympathy. Sympathy draws the other person closer. Empathy repels and irritates. Empathy increases shame. Empathy helps you overcome shame. This is why most people dislike being empathized with and despise those who do. Empathy does not cause negative emotions and helps people feel that they are not alone with these problems.
The first way to show empathy is to say that many of your clients have faced and dealt with the same problems, and you are trying to help them with everything. "Many of our clients feel the same way.

But together, we have come to the conclusion that your problem can be solved in the following ways...."
Don't take other people's problems lightly. Inexperienced salespeople, when they realize what the customer's problem is, rush to say, "Sorry. That's okay. We've already solved your problem." Everything feels right. They emphasize that the company has faced similar problems many times before and has the knowledge and skills to solve it as quickly as possible. Or is it not that simple? What is the problem here? The salesperson is not paying attention to the customer's pain. If the problem is not very serious, you can solve it.

That's fine. But what if the problem hasn't been solved for a long time, and another company couldn't help him? His first reaction will be, "I see, this idiot doesn't realize the seriousness of the problem. In this case, the salesperson should have been more careful and said, "I can imagine how inconvenient this is for you. Obviously, this is not an easy situation. But we have dealt with similar issues before. I can assure you that all of our customers have been very satisfied. This is a more acceptable way to say it.

People are driven first by emotion and then by logic. As a result, they may not realize that their actions are hurting themselves. A customer may turn down a very good deal just because the salesperson used condescending language. Avoid such mistakes. Learn to think differently. That's what makes us masters of sales.

## Chapter 9.

## The Most Common Objection You Give Up On.

The most common objection you hear all the time is. "We don't have any money." Let's try to find out what's wrong with this objection. The real reason is this. People don't know how to afford it. Nobody can afford to buy anything unless they need it. Once the priorities in a person's life change, somehow people find the money to go on vacation to the islands, buy another car, and send their child to private school. No matter how poor you are, you're not living under a bridge and spending $10,000 a year. What do you spend that money on? Some of it goes to living expenses, but some of it goes to priorities. So you have to ask yourself, is it really true that they don't have money?

It's just that people don't know what they want. People just don't know how to want and get what they want. And you, as a master salesman, should paint a picture of a person's whole life, his future, and what he will get if he solves his problems. The more colorful and detailed you describe the future that will happen after the person solves his problem, the stronger the desire will be to solve that problem. The problem is not that the person doesn't have money and can't afford it - it's just that the person doesn't prioritize it. But if it is a priority and it is necessary, the money is there. And the main task of a sales master is to teach a person to afford to solve this - their long-standing and unpleasant problem, to afford to buy this service or product.

Customers perceive a product as expensive when they simply do not understand why it costs so much. In other words, either the value of the product is not being communicated correctly, or ther is no value in the product at all. You need to understand what people are paying money for in the first place.

Indeed, "selling by pain point" is very convenient. But it is not a panacea. What pain do flower shops or golf clubs address? And a lot of restaurants develop because consumers are hungry, or there are other ways to add value.

Time is of the essence. Is shopping online really better? You can't try the product on, touch it, or judge its quality. And there are scammers at every turn. Yet online shopping continues. We're talking about online shopping where shoppers can make their own choices. People buy everything online, from clothes to transportation. The choice is between spending half a day shopping or ordering everything they need in a few clicks. If your product saves customers time, they will never give it up. And you should talk about it. Also, don't make the buying process too cumbersome. If you have to go to a bank branch or find a payment system terminal instead of swiping a bank card to pay, it's just not convenient and the buyer will reject such a purchase.

Entertainment. Artists fill stadiums and do not solve your problems. This activity is not new. People like to be entertained, but they also like complicity, games and jokes. That's why even banks today are using mobile apps to make it easy for their customers to pay utility bills and transfer money.

You have to make it fun to use the product. People like to take coupons for grocery shopping, to get an unwanted set of cutlery, or to get a themed toy for a child.

Incentive. Some "gurus" make millions of dollars by telling people what everyone already knows. Many life-changing decisions lie on the surface. Quitting smoking, going to school, eating less, or not quitting a job you hate. But the one who finds the right words and motivates you to get off the couch is the one you're willing to pay. What's more attractive - an offer to train for an in-demand job or a new life you've been dreaming about for so long? What's more powerful - a request to submit a job application or a nudge to take a life-changing step?

Show the customer they are special. People like to have something that no one else has. "Limited edition" sells faster and at a higher price. You'll get more response by offering your products to a limited number of special customers, not everyone. That's not the only way to make your customers feel unique. Emphasize that your services are already being used by celebrities. Advertising always works. Always emphasize that your product is for the elite.

Simplicity. This is the foundation of the entire information industry. It pays to talk about complex things in simple terms. If your product or service makes life simpler and easier to understand, customers will flow in. You should use these principles to deliver information in concise, simple, uncomplicated language.

Feel free to combine these techniques. Remember that many leading brands do this in seemingly contradictory ways. For example, they save time and provide entertainment. They say that even a child can use it, but insist that the product is for a select few. All to increase the value of the product in the minds of customers.

How to maximize your effectiveness.
It happens all the time. In a conversation with a customer he says: "I like everything, but send me all this to my e-mail". First of all, you have to prepare everything, if you have something ready, you have to finalize it to meet the needs of this customer. This person is not going to buy from you and you're wasting your time. So you ask, "If I send you these materials, what happens next?" "I'll think about it, I'll talk to my partner." And you just ask, "If you get these materials from me with the price quoted. How long will it take you to discuss it and make a decision? Can you afford to buy our product?" You write it all down in your notebook. "These are the terms we discussed with you, are they suitable for you? Then we can move forward, right? I'll send all the paperwork today and when will you come to sign the contract? What date, what time? I'll write it all down so we don't get in the way. If the client agrees, you can start preparing the necessary materials and send them to him. He's already agreed to buy what you're offering. All you have to do is spell out all these terms in your contract. But a piece of paper isn't enough. It won't close the deal, it won't solve the customer's problem.

If you don't find a problem that your product, your piece of paper, can solve, it won't close the deal. A deal has to be closed with the right communication. If it were that simple, you wouldn't need anything more than a website. Where all the offers can be printed out and easily downloaded to your phone. You could charge it directly to your card or pay online. But for some reason, it doesn't happen. Why not? Because the website can't ask the right questions, can't detect problems.

Your job is to send contracts and offers to someone who is ready to pay, the price suits them, they have money and they are ready to work with you. A large number of salespeople fail at almost every offer they make. This happens because they don't realize that they need to be prepared. Even a perfectly crafted text won't replace a master salesman. But by now you'll know how to maximize your effectiveness. There's no substitute for live communication, not just in sales, but in almost any field. This is especially true when you need expert advice.

Here are some tips for creating a script that works.

Don't rely too much on written text, but that doesn't mean you should forget about it altogether. Yes, you're in sales, and the sales pitch is still important. But boring, bland or dry proposals, even after the most inspiring presentation, can sabotage results and derail the deal. Besides, no one is going to turn down a client who prefers to read a document rather than talk on the phone. However, the entire appeal of the product lies in the commercial proposition. This means that all aspects must be well thought out.

Title and introduction. This is the first thing the customer sees and the most important text explaining the essence of what will be discussed next. They are the main factors that determine whether a cold customer will read your proposal. They are also the only chance for a hot customer to make a repeat first impression. This means you need to choose phrases that are meaningful and apt. Here are some of the most appropriate ways to make headlines memorable. Numbers. "Five reasons to contact us." Questions. "How much money do you need to be happy?

Audience. Special offer for mothers with small children.

References. "A promotion that will surprise you. Wordplay." Buying your first swimming lesson will make you feel like a slave in the water everywhere'". The key is not to lose sight of the content. A good opening should address the customer's problem and paint a rosy picture of what will happen if the deal is done. As a general rule, the first paragraph should contain the most important information. Of course, it can also be intriguing. But that requires skill on the part of the writer. Also, it won't be as effective for someone who's already been on the phone with you.

Formatting. First impressions are made by the way you dress. Even if they've only heard of you or only interacted with you on the phone. They'll still notice the attractive look of your presentation. About 70 percent of the world's business proposals are sent over the Internet. Designs are more about efficiency than effectiveness. Designs can favorably emphasize and highlight the key details of your product, highlight pain points, and offer a solution to a problem.

Proposal. Describe your product and the benefits to customers of working with you. Forget long sentences and vague promises. Be as specific and bite-sized as possible. Whatever the proposal is, it's worth including the benefits of your product or service.

Respond quickly. You and I don't like to wait. But more than anything, people don't like uncertainty. So instead of saying, "We'll get back to you as soon as possible," say, "We'll get back to you within 3-5 days.

Simple payments. The more payment methods you have, the more likely you are to do business with any customer in any country. If you can offer installment payments, the possibilities are even greater. Warranty: "Return if you don't like it within 14 days", "Repair and maintenance for 24 months". These guarantees are backed up by documentation, which makes the decision-making process easier for the buyer.

Variety. Even if there is only one product, give customers a variety of choices. Remember the "three box" strategy. Customers like to pay for what they choose, not what they are forced to pay for. Discounts and Giveaways "The week before and after Black Friday, we offer 20% off all merchandise. "If you buy today, we will give you a discount coupon for a second visit. The first strategy is designed to increase sales now, and the second strategy is designed to increase sales in the near future.

Anticipate objections. Put yourself in the customer's shoes and understand what might be bothering them. Think of situations where the product is a scam, the price seems too high, or there are other objections. Now think about what motivated you to pay for the product. Most likely it's: "Testimonial" - written by a real person. Pictures that look like real people. Talking about typical fears and showing real results.

Trial period. Businesses that are gaining momentum, such as online courses and services, use this to attract new customers. They have the opportunity to try and pay later. If you're selling a product rather than a service, you need samples to try. Value is much bigger than price. It's not hard to strike a balance between "nothing unique" and "too good to be true. Of course, an attractive and realistic offer will always get attention. If that offer is limited in time, it will be even more compelling.

By the way, there is a small problem: people often think that the purpose of a commercial offer is obvious and that it should work anyway, but it doesn't. In business, repetition is the mother of sales. Therefore, a call to action is not superfluous. If you don't keep these and other tips in mind, you will lose the battle with your customers.

## Chapter 10.
## What does it mean to milk a customer?

I'm going to let you in on a sales secret. Whoever has a greater desire to help their customer wins. If you have a truly useful product or service that will help solve a person's problem.

Only 5% of people are ready to buy your product right now. They need what you're selling. There's another 10% of people who want it, but they don't know how to do it, they've thought about it, but they're not ready. And another 30% of people basically need your services but haven't heard of you or even know that their problem can be solved. And 55 percent of those aren't interested in your product.

If your product is expensive, that five percent is enough. Because they are looking for you. In that case, you can make more money than the average salesperson. But our job is to learn how to sell to the other 10 percent of people and the 30 percent of people who want to buy but don't even know the service exists.

That's where the talent is. Show the person a real problem and find a solution. From the 30 percent who don't even know their problem is solvable, you move happily to the 5 percent who are ready to buy right now.

It's about saving this person. And it won't be unreasonable to remind them of your service or product. You've written down all their wishes in your notebook. And now it's time for a new procedure, a product with similar characteristics is released, new developments that solve the customer's pain and problem.

You have to remember. And in a short time your sales will increase significantly. The whole point is that you have started to think and are not afraid to offer the customer what he needs and what he is waiting for.

That's why people who want to help another person or customer win in business and sales. And then people start to appreciate and respect you. That's why you can't cheat your customers. Everything has to be followed through to the end. In the end, you have to help him and do everything possible to make his life better. Remember, you are not forcing anyone to do anything. You show them that there is a better and more interesting life out there. Then you don't have to worry about sales. Knowing how to properly "milk" your customers is always an advantage. After all, your sales may be 55% of your potential customers. Sales masters never waste time on unlikely customers, but they also never miss an opportunity to close a deal. All of the techniques described here have been used since ancient times. These are extremely effective methods used as a weapon by a true master salesman.

Sometimes you need to look simple. A little false naiveté can reassure customers who suspect you of pushing inappropriate goods. Avoiding relevant topics and explanations can make the customer feel superior. Then, as the customer relaxes, you can begin to gently nudge them in the right direction. But do not cross the line into incompetence.

Ask questions carefully. Not all business can be done in one call. Conduct "conversations" intelligently. Elicit information from the client that they would not normally share with a stranger. Use it somewhere near the end of the deal. So it's not clear where you're being sneaky. Asking questions after you say goodbye can catch them off guard. Also, since they've mentally left the conversation, they'll want to answer the question as soon as possible. When these circumstances combine, the customer is almost certain to spill the beans. Then use that information in a future meeting. "Everybody lies." People who swear to tell the truth lie more than others. Inexperienced salespeople give up when they hear phrases like, "I can't buy right now," "I'm fine with my business partner," or "I'll think about it and get back to you. This is the potential buyer saying, in plain and simple language, that they are not buying anything right now. "There's no way you're lying. No, it's possible." Ninety percent of the objections you hear are lies. Some customers lie to get a discount. For example, they say they love everything, but they can only pay 80% of your price because they are already on a budget. In many cases, however, it's a lie to be polite. Usually, conflict causes unpleasant psychological feelings for people. But "Thanks for the information, it was helpful, I'll get back to you" sounds acceptable. Working with these clients requires directness. If they say they will think about it and get back to you, never contact them. "You and I both know that's just a polite rejection. If our product isn't right for you, just say so. We won't take offense." When you say this, the customer gets lost and gives you a truthful reason.

As a master salesperson, you know what you have to work with. You and I are lucky to have you. With this knowledge, nothing is impossible. Experiment more and don't be afraid to fail. Especially now as you learn to be a Master Salesperson.

The customer delays the purchase, what to do.
I'm going to talk about how a customer delays a purchase. If the person doesn't need a life change, then you don't just hang up the phone, you hang up the phone very quickly. What I mean is this. The vocabulary of the person trying to talk to you includes words like "Maybe," "Later," "Sometime later," "Sometime after that," "I'm not ready yet..." That time will never come. Your job is to help successful people become more successful. That's the only way your income will increase. It's not your job to help people who don't want to change. But if a person wants to improve his life and his situation, he will come to you. He comes to you and you change the situation, remove the problem that is holding him back.

Others are not worth wasting your time on. Because they just occupy your life 24 hours a day, every day. You lose your mood, you lose your energy. When you hear that the person is not ready, you say, "Thank you for telling me. It's important to me. Don't work with people like that. You can help those who want to help themselves. Intuition will always help you, it's that feeling you have inside. You know immediately who you're talking to. But to get to that level, you have to get experience.

It takes practice. But you've been doing the same thing for years and you're getting the same results. So it's time to change your tactics. It's time to learn how to say no to clients. The hardest word to say is only three letters long. You still haven't learned how to say "no" in life and in business. You need to know how to say no. Not only to procrastinators, but also to greedy, arrogant, complaining, and other problem customers. These simple tips will make your job easier.

Offer alternative solutions. Customer requests can sometimes be overwhelming. A customer asks for a 30% discount for no reason. Or thinks it's your responsibility to provide the product for free. You don't have to follow their lead. Nor do you have the right to pander to these customers. But you can try to defuse the situation. You can't give them what they want. But you can give him a rewards card that gives him 5% off his next purchase. That's probably not what he wanted. But you did offer a nice bonus. And that's more than a no. Will that stop a boring man? No. But a decent man wouldn't be mad at you. In short, you didn't turn him down, you made him an offer he could take. Which he turned down. Now it's his move, as they say.

Offer a price with the buyer in mind, not yourself. Consider the same situation: if you answer that a 30% discount is not possible, most buyers will ask why not. Ninety percent of the time, the salesperson will reply that the company can't afford it. This is a classic mistake. Think about it. The buyer doesn't care what your company does.

He doesn't care how much it costs to buy your product, how much your employees are paid, how much your rent is, and how much it costs to sedate people like him. You can tell him all the numbers in detail, but don't expect him to understand or sympathize. So think of the benefits to him, not your costs. "This product is very expensive. We package it carefully so that you receive it in the best possible condition. Delivery is fast and always on time. We offer a guarantee and will advise you on any questions you may have. If necessary, we will solve any problems within the specified time frame. Our product and service are worth every dollar.

Arguments for closing. Contrary to popular belief, the customer is almost always wrong. His claims are often unbelievable or at least questionable. Without understanding the nature of the problem, he manages to blame you for all fatal misdeeds. Even if they are mistakes of his own choosing. To get the client to start listening to you on principle. Just ask for specifics and you can break down his arguments. "Didn't we remind you that this product can only be returned within 14 days?" "Which of our tips didn't work for you?" "What exactly did you do to the unit when it stopped working?" After a few polite questions, your position will be strengthened. Now allow the customer to be specific about their complaint. For example, "Your product is terrible" often means they don't like the color of the product. Or they expected it to have features you didn't mention. Or they expected to see results after a few days of training and you promised months.

Hearing "no" out of the blue is very different from hearing "no" when you analyze a customer's real statements for real arguments.

Never be deceptive. Many salespeople tend to say nonsense to avoid saying "no." This usually only complicates the situation. If the customer insists, your meaningless "maybe" will start to sound like "yes. "We sympathize with your situation, but we don't sell training at half price, much less offer it for free to someone who promises a refund later. Keep an eye on our website for events. We run specials from time to time. In the meantime, start with some basic free video training. This is usually the answer people get when they want to improve their figure for free. They will not only state the case, but also make other suggestions. There is not a single person who will curse and resent you after such a dialog.

In most cases, however, customers don't give up after one "no." You need to say these words in the same polite and confident tone every time. "No, everything has already been explained", "I refuse again", "No, this option is impossible" .... Memorizing these phrases will save you a lot of time and effort.

The word "No" is the most honest thing you can say to a customer. You must realize that over time, deals are either made on favorable terms or broken on unfavorable terms. In other words, you will win either way. I would add that the more often you start saying "no" to uncertain people, the more often you will hear "yes" from the right people.